PRINCIPLES OF COGNITIVE PSYCHOLOGY

MICHAEL W. EYSENCK

A volume in the series
Principles of Psychology

Series Editors
Michael W. Eysenck
Simon Green
Nicky Hayes

 LAWRENCE ERLBAUM ASSOCIATES, PUBLISHERS
Hove (UK)   Hillsdale (USA)

Reprinted 1993

Lawrence Erlbaum Associates Ltd., Publishers
27 Palmeira Mansions
Church Road
Hove
East Sussex, BN3 2FA
U.K.

British Library Cataloguing in Publication Data

A catalogue record for this book is available from the British Library

ISBN 0-86377-252-8 (hbk)
ISBN 0-86377-253-6 (pbk)

Cartoons by Sanz
Subject index compiled by Jackie McDermott
Cover design by Stuart Walden
Printed and bound by Redwood Books, Trowbridge

Contents

To my wife Christine, with love

Preface

Of all the major areas within psychology, it is probably cognitive psychology which has seen the greatest increase in research and theory over the past decade or so. This has happened in terms of both basic and applied research. Basic research in cognitive psychology is concerned with the processes and structures involved in, for example, attention, perception, learning, memory, language, and reasoning. Applied research in cognitive psychology is concerned with the ways in which these basic processes and structures are used by different groups in different settings. For example, as cognitive therapists have argued for many years, it is possible to devise effective methods of treatment for depression and anxiety by considering the cognitive processes of clinical patients in those emotional states.

This book is largely concerned with our understanding of basic cognitive processes. There have been major advances in recent years in most of the areas of cognitive psychology discussed in this book, and the outlook for the future looks very promising. While the major focus is on basic cognitive functions, practical applications of research are not neglected. As will become clear while reading this book, cognitive psychologists are increasingly concerned to carry out research which has real implications for the understanding of everyday life.

This book is appropriately dedicated to my wife. She has had to cope with a husband who sometimes seems to be wedded to his word processor, but she has put up with the trials and tribulations involved with good humour and tolerance. Without her support, this book would not have been written.

What is cognitive psychology?

1

A s this entire book is devoted to cognitive psychology, it is appropriate to set the scene by describing in some detail exactly what we mean by cognitive psychology. This is easier said than done for a variety of reasons. Cognitive psychologists favour different theoretical approaches, and investigate a wide range of phenomena, and it can be difficult to describe their endeavours in a coherent fashion. Despite this, we will attempt to impose a structure on the subject of cognitive psychology.

Most cognitive psychologists agree that the subject matter of cognitive psychology consists of the main internal psychological processes that are involved in making sense of the environment. These processes include attention, perception, learning, memory, language, concept formation, problem solving, and thinking.

The other side of the coin is that cognitive psychologists are generally *not* interested in physiological psychology, individual differences, or social psychology. The term "cognition" was used long ago by philosophers who divided psychology into three components: cognition, conation, and affect. "Conation" is similar in meaning to "motivation", and "affect" means "emotion"—it is still the case today that those who investigate cognition tend to avoid the topics of motivation and emotion.

Cognitive psychologists agree in a general sense that one of the major goals of cognitive psychology is to provide precise accounts of the internal processes that are involved in the performance of cognitive tasks. As we will see later on, there is some disagreement about the best way of attaining that goal, but there is a reasonable consensus on the purpose of cognitive psychology.

Perhaps we can most easily understand the approach favoured by cognitive psychologists if we look at a concrete example. Consider the letter-transformation task that was used by Hockey and his associates (Hockey, MacLean, & Hamilton, 1981). Between one and four letters are presented in this task, and each letter has to be transformed by working a specified distance through the alphabet (see the examples alongside): In every case, the answer has to be given as a single response. If subjects are

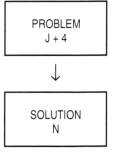

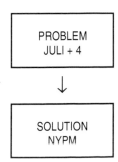

given a reasonable amount of practice, then they make relatively few errors. What is of interest is the length of time taken to solve each problem.

The basic findings with this task are relatively straightforward. Solution time lengthens as the number of letters per problem increases. One would expect four-letter problems to take longer than one-letter problems, but they actually take much more than four times as long to solve. The difficulty of the letter- transformation task is clearly affected more than we might have expected by an increase in the number of letters in the problem because of the growing demands on short-term memory. Why? Various avenues were explored.

For example, Hockey et al. (1981) looked at the effects of white noise—intense, meaningless noise—on this task, but discovered that it did not affect total response time. What else could be done in order to clarify what is actually going on in this task? The answer provided by Hockey et al. (1981) was to identify the processes involved, and then to sub-divide the total solution time into component times based on these processes. They identified three processing stages for each letter:

- An *encoding stage*, in which the appropriate part of the alphabet is located in long-term memory;
- A *transformation stage*, in which the letter is transformed;
- A *storage stage*, in which the accumulating answer is rehearsed and stored in memory.

As these three processing stages are repeated with each successive letter, it follows that 4-letter problems consist of a total of 12 processing stages. By requiring the subjects to press a button to see each letter in turn, and asking them to perform the transformations out loud, Hockey et al. (1981) were able to divide the solution time for 4-letter problems into 12 component times. The increased demands on memory as the subjects worked through four-letter problems letter-by-letter had only marginal effects on the encoding and transformation stages, but lengthened the storage stage. Thus, four-letter problems are difficult largely because of the storage demands imposed. Hockey et al. (1981) also found that the lack of any effect of white noise on total solution time was misleading. White noise speeded up the transformation time, but it slowed down the storage time. This suggests that white noise enables simple tasks to be performed faster, but reduces the efficiency of a short-term memory system that holds information over short periods of time.

Before the growth of cognitive psychology in the late 1950s and early 1960s, researchers would almost certainly have been content to measure only total solution times, and they would have refused to speculate on the processes involved. I hope you will agree that the cognitive psychological approach adopted by Hockey et al. (1981) provides a much more insightful account. In particular, the earlier approach would have led to the conclusion that white noise had no effect at all on the letter-transformation task, which we can now see is quite untrue.

Information-processing theory

Most cognitive psychologists adopt what is often referred to as the *information-processing approach* (see Lachman, Lachman, & Butterfield, 1979). Some of the major assumptions of the information-processing approach are as follows:

- Information made available by the environment is processed by a series of processing systems (e.g. attention, perception, short-term memory).
- These processing systems transform or alter the information in various systematic ways (e.g. three connected lines are presented to our eyes, but we see a triangle).
- The aim of research is to specify the processes and structures (e.g. long-term memory) that underlie cognitive performance.
- Information processing in people resembles that in computers.

A version of the information-processing approach that was popular approximately 25 years ago is shown in the diagram on the right. According to this version, a stimulus (an environmental event such as a problem or task) is presented to the subject, and this stimulus causes certain internal cognitive processes to occur. These processes ultimately produce the required response or answer. Processing directly affected by the stimulus input is usually described as *stimulus-driven* or *bottom-up processing*. In addition, it is assumed by this version of information-processing theory that only one process occurs at any one moment in time. This is known as *serial processing*, and means that one process is completed before the next begins. Some of the reasons why this version of information-processing theory is no longer popular are discussed in the following pages

Bottom-up versus top-down processing

There is no dispute about the importance of bottom-up or stimulus-driven processing in cognition. However, it is generally agreed nowadays that this is not the whole story. What is left out is what the individual brings to the task in terms of his or her expectations and past experience. These influences constitute *top-down* or *conceptually driven processing*. Look at the triangle overleaf, and read what it says.

STIMULUS

↓

| attention |

↓

| perception |

↓

| thought processes |

↓

| decision |

↓

RESPONSE OR ACTION

Unless you are familiar with this trick, you will probably read it as "Paris in the spring". Look again and you will see that "the" is repeated. What happens is that your expectation that it is the well-known phrase (i.e. top-down processing) overrides the information actually available in the stimulus (i.e. bottom-up processing).

It is now widely accepted that most cognition involves a mixture of bottom-up and top-down processing. An especially clear illustration of this comes from a study by Bruner and Postman (1949) in which people expected to see conventional playing cards presented very briefly. When black hearts were presented, some of the subjects claimed to have seen purple or brown hearts. Here we have an almost literal blending of the black colour stemming from bottom-up processing and of the red colour stemming from top-down processing, due to the expectation that hearts will be red.

Serial versus parallel processing

The notion that processing is serial (i.e. one process is completed before the next starts) is illustrated by the letter-transformation task described earlier. It is obvious that a letter cannot be transformed until the relevant part of the alphabet has been located, and that the results of the transformation cannot be rehearsed until the transformation is complete. The encoding, transformation, and storage stages must therefore follow each other in serial fashion.

A very different possibility is that some or all of the processes involved in a cognitive task occur at the same time. This is known as *parallel processing*. In view of the brain's processing power, it seems likely that parallel processing is often used during thinking and problem solving. A third possibility is that tasks are handled by a mixture of serial and parallel processing. In other words, some processes can occur together, but other processes must await the completion of earlier processes.

It is probably unwise to be dogmatic on the issue of the relative importance of serial and parallel processing in cognitive functioning. It is actually rather difficult to determine whether a particular task is being processed in a serial or a parallel fashion. Let us reconsider the letter-transformation task. While, as we have just argued, it must involve serial processing, that does not rule out the possibility that parallel processing is also involved. Perhaps subjects continue to rehearse and to store the accumulating answer while they are encoding and transforming the later letters in the problem: we just do not know.

It is virtually certain that whether serial or parallel processing predominates depends crucially on the particular processes required to solve a given problem or task. Of particular importance, as we will see in Chapter 3, is the amount of practice that an individual has had on a particular task. Parallel processing occurs much more frequently when someone is highly skilled than when they are just beginning to master a skill. For example, a skilled typist can be thinking several letters ahead while typing, whereas a novice typist focuses on just one letter at a time.

Brains and computers

One way of trying to make sense of something we do not understand very well, much used by scientists and others, is to relate or compare it to something we do understand. This is known as argument by analogy, and it goes back thousands of years. For example, Socrates compared long-term memory to an aviary, with the pieces of information we possess being represented by birds. Remembering was compared to hunting for a particular bird, and errors in remembering were likened to catching hold of a bird that resembled the one sought in some way. Since then, as Henry Roediger (1980) has pointed out, the memory system has been compared to all sorts of things. Technological advances have played an important role, so that Socrates's analogy based on aviaries has been replaced by analogies involving gramophones, tape recorders, conveyor belts, and even underground maps. As part and parcel of this trend, many cognitive psychologists in recent years have been impressed by an analogy between human cognition and computer functioning. Computers can be regarded as information-processing systems. They combine the information presented to them with the information that they already have stored to provide solutions to an enormous variety of problems. At a superficial level, this sounds very much like the way in which people solve problems.

There are other similarities between human brains and computers. For example, most computers have a central processor of limited capacity, and it is usually assumed that capacity limitations also affect the human attentional system (see Chapter 3). However, most computers until comparatively recently have only been programmed to function in a serial fashion, whereas the human brain has the capacity for extensive parallel processing. A further difference is that people are often influenced in their thinking by a number of conflicting emotional and motivational forces, which contrasts markedly with the "single-minded nature of virtually all current computer programs" (Boden, 1988, p. 262).

There is some disagreement among cognitive psychologists about how far we should take the computer analogy. It is clear that computers and people are both symbol systems in the sense that external and internal events are symbolised, and the resultant symbols are then manipulated in various ways. Some cognitive psychologists have gone much further, especially those working in the area of cognitive science or artificial intelligence. These workers have claimed that computer and human cognition resemble each other very closely, and they have gone on to develop computer programs that mimic the performance of people in various cognitive tasks. The argument is that such programs can potentially be of great use in helping to explain how people handle these tasks.

The debate as to the ultimate usefulness of the computer analogy continues. For present purposes, it is important to note that the information-processing approach developed by cognitive psychologists owes much to the perceived similarity between the cognitive functioning of people and of computers. Furthermore, as advocates of the computer metaphor have pointed out, because computers are flexible, we can realistically hope that the differences between human and computer functioning will be reduced in the years to come.

Damaged brains and cognition

One way of trying to understand the human information-processing system is by studying brain-damaged patients. This is precisely what *cognitive neuropsychologists* do. They assume that the cognitive system consists of several *modules* or cognitive processors within the brain. These modules operate relatively independently of each other, so that brain damage can impair the functioning of some modules while leaving other modules intact. Thus, for example, the modules or processors involved in understanding speech are presumably rather different from those involved in actually speaking. As a consequence, there are some brain-damaged patients who are good at language comprehension but poor at speaking, and others who show the opposite pattern.

Many of the patients studied by cognitive neuropsychologists suffer from puzzling and intriguing problems. Consider, for example, the case of patients with "blindsight". These are patients who are blind in part of the visual field—they have no conscious awareness of objects presented to that part.

Surprisingly, they can still make accurate judgements about visual stimuli presented to the apparently "blind" part of the visual field. The patient DB, who was examined by Weiskrantz (1986), was able to detect whether or not a visual stimulus had been presented to his blind area, and he could also identify its location. An implication of work on blindsight is that we need to rethink our views on perception. While we normally regard visual perception as depending crucially on conscious awareness, the evidence from blindsight patients suggests that a considerable amount of perceptual processing occurs in the absence of conscious awareness.

Cognitive neuropsychologists try to understand how the cognitive system works by looking for what are known as *dissociations*. A dissociation occurs when a patient performs at the normal level on one task but is severely impaired on a second task. For example, many amnesic patients perform well on tasks involving short-term memory but exhibit very poor performance on long-term memory tasks (see Chapter 4). This suggests that short-term memory and long-term memory involve separate modules. It could be argued, on the other hand, that brain damage reduces the ability to perform difficult (but not easy) tasks, and that long-term memory tasks are more difficult than short-term memory tasks. It has also been discovered, however, that some brain-damaged patients have good long-term memory but impaired short-term memory. Thus, it seems reasonable to assume that separate modules or cognitive processors are involved in short-term and long-term memory.

The memory research which has just been discussed illustrates a *double dissociation*. A double dissociation between two tasks occurs when some patients perform task A normally but are impaired on task B, whereas other patients perform task B normally but are impaired on task A. It is generally agreed that double dissociations provide the strongest evidence for the existence of separate modules.

The cognitive neuropsychological approach assumes that the cognitive performance exhibited by brain-damaged patients provides direct information about the impact of brain damage on previously normal cognitive systems. There are, however, at least two reasons why such an assumption may be unwarranted. First, at least some brain-damaged patients may have had somewhat unusual cognitive systems prior to brain damage. Second, some of the impact of brain damage on cognitive functioning may be camouflaged because patients develop compensatory strategies designed to help them cope with their brain damage. If that happens, it becomes much harder to make sense of their cognitive impairments.

Perspectives on information processing

- The information-processing approach is the one that has been used by most cognitive psychologists. It claims that various complex processes occur between the presentation of a stimulus (e.g. an anagram problem) and the subsequent response (e.g. the solution to the anagram). These processes involve transforming the presented information in a number of ways in order to perform the task in question.
- Within the information-processing approach, there have been disagreements about the relative importance of bottom-up and top-down processing, and about the extent to which processing is serial or parallel.
- There has been controversy about the degree of similarity between the functioning of the human brain and that of the computer. There is fairly general agreement, however, that both are information-processing systems. While the human brain often engages in parallel processing, most computer programs function in a serial fashion.
- Cognitive neuropsychologists argue that we can understand cognitive functioning by considering brain-damaged patients. Brain damage impairs the functioning of only certain aspects of cognition, and a study of the pattern of impairment can tell us about the organisation of the cognitive system.

The real world

Cognitive psychologists, at least until fairly recently, have been mainly interested in studying cognition under laboratory conditions. Experiments carried out under such conditions are typically tightly controlled and "scientific". The findings are, therefore, relatively easy to make sense of and to interpret. There are, however, some real drawbacks with this approach. The most obvious problem is that data and theories based on laboratory research may not be applicable to the world outside. As cognitive psychologists have become more aware of this problem, they have increasingly argued that research should possess *ecological validity*—i.e. it should be of relevance to everyday events and concerns.

One of the best-known advocates of the importance of ecological validity is Ulric Neisser (1976). He launched an attack on much laboratory- based research, arguing that cognitive psychologists should make "a greater effort to understand cognition as it occurs in the ordinary environment and in the context of natural purposeful activity" [p. 7]. It might seem that one way of following Neisser's advice would be to study cognition only in everyday settings.

Unfortunately this approach has its own limitations, in particular the difficulty of establishing proper experimental control. What is needed is a fruitful exchange of ideas and data between researchers investigating cognition in laboratory and in applied settings. Laboratory research has produced reliable data and many interesting theories, and their general significance can be ascertained in everyday settings. In other words, research in everyday settings provides an appropriate way of *testing* the usefulness of data and theories emerging from the laboratory.

Most cognitive psychologists agree that the ideal is a combination of experimental rigour and ecological validity. This ideal can at present best be approximated by considering the same cognitive skills in the laboratory and in everyday settings. When the realistic but relatively messy data of everyday life are broadly in line with the somewhat artificial but pure data of the laboratory, then we may have some confidence that we are making genuine progress in probing the mysteries of human cognition.

At this point, it is worth illustrating how cognitive psychology can be of practical relevance. Consider, for example, what might be done in order to improve the reading skills of children with very poor reading comprehension. Palincsar and Brown (1984) noticed that much standard laboratory research had indicated that good readers are much better than poor readers at identifying the major themes within a text, and that identification of the major themes facilitates the reading process. Accordingly, they argued that reading skills might improve if poor readers were given training specifically designed to permit rapid discovery of the main theme. They trained poor readers to identify the central theme by asking them to think about the structure of the texts they were reading, and to ask appropriate questions about each text. This simple teaching programme produced a marked improvement, with the reading comprehension of the children ultimately being well above the average for children of their age.

Another example concerns the information obtained from eyewitnesses to crimes. Laboratory research on memory suggested that they might remember more if they were able to recreate the context at the time of the crime, to repeat the events from different perspectives, and to report the crime in a number of different orders. When these and other suggestions were incorporated into interviews, eye-witnesses were able to remember almost 50% more than in the standard police interview (Fisher, Geiselman, Raymond, Jurkenich, & Warhaytig, 1987).

Summary: What is cognitive psychology?

- Cognitive psychology is the study of the processes involved in cognition—the processes involved in making sense of the environment and interacting appropriately with it.
- The information-processing approach attempts to understand the number and nature of the internal psychological processes that intervene between the presentation of a stimulus and the subsequent response. These processes may occur one after the other (i.e. serial processing) or they may occur together (i.e. parallel processing).
- Bottom-up processes are initiated almost entirely by the stimulus. Top-down processes are affected by the individual's knowledge and expectations. Most theoretical accounts of cognition try to specify the extent to which the processes involved in a cognitive task are serial or parallel, bottom-up or top-down.
- Computers and people both process information, and the information-processing approach favoured by cognitive psychologists makes use of the apparent similarities between computers and people. The ultimate value of regarding people as unusually complex computers remains the subject of lively debate.
- One of the long-term goals of cognitive psychology is to provide an understanding of cognitive functioning that has practical applications. There are many common cases of cognitive malfunctioning that might potentially benefit from the accumulated knowledge of cognitive psychology; these include special problems in learning to read and poor memory. Cognitive psychologists have tended in the past to focus on somewhat narrow topics studied under laboratory conditions, but strenuous attempts are now being made to make cognitive psychology of practical relevance to the everyday world.

Further reading

Most of the topics discussed in this chapter are dealt with in more detail in M. W. Eysenck and M. T. Keane (1990), *Cognitive Psychology: A Student's Handbook* (Hove, UK: Lawrence Erlbaum Associates Ltd.). The information-processing approach is discussed fully by Lachman, Lachman, and Butterfield (1979), *Cognitive Psychology and Information Processing* (Hillsdale, NJ: Lawrence Erlbaum Associates Inc.). Cognitive neuropsychology is discussed very fully by A. W. Ellis and A. W. Young (1988), *Human Cognitive Neuropsychology* (Hove, UK: Lawrence Erlbaum Associates Ltd.).

Sensory systems and perception

2

What is perception? As a starting point, we will adopt the definition proposed by Levine and Shefner (1981): "Perception refers to the way in which we interpret the information gathered (and processed) by the senses. In a word, we sense the presence of a stimulus, but we perceive what it is" [p. 1]. This definition embraces both aspects of perception—that it depends upon sensations (based on basic sensory information), but that these sensations require interpretation in order for perception to occur.

There are several complex processes involved in the interpretation of sensory information, cutting across the fields of both psychology and physiology. Some of the physiological processes and systems are discussed in the next section, and more psychological processes are dealt with in the rest of the chapter.

Perception is a large topic and whole books have been written about it. Our coverage is inevitably rather selective. We concentrate on visual perception and, to a lesser extent, auditory perception, and have little to say about other senses. Why? First, vision and hearing are the sense modalities which we use to explore the environment, and which are therefore of most general signficance in everyday life. Second, there is much evidence that the visual sense is the dominant one for most purposes. In one study, for example, James Gibson (1933) asked subjects to run their hands along a straight edge while wearing optical equipment that made straight edges appear to be curved. The subjects consistently reported that the straight edge felt as if it was curved, thus demonstrating that a conflict between visual and touch information is resolved in favour of visual information. Third, very much more is known about perception in the visual and auditory modalities than in any of the other sense modalities.

Sensory systems

The basic physiological systems associated with the sense modalities are relevant to psychologists in a number of ways. For example, the limitations of our sensory systems impose restrictions on our perceptual powers. We cannot hear dog whistles because our auditory physiological system is not equipped to respond to sounds of such high frequency. Similarly, colour blindness is usually caused by deficiencies in cone pigment in the retina of the eye.

The processes involved in using any of the sense modalities have common characteristics. First of all, a stimulus (e.g. the page you are reading) affects the sense receptor that is designed to detect it (in this case, the eye). The energy changes produced by this stimulus at the receptor are then converted or transduced into neural impulses which retain the stimulus information. The information contained within the neural impulses is then transmitted to the higher levels of the central nervous system, where it combines with relevant knowledge stored in long-term memory to provide us with conscious awareness of the original stimulus (i.e. allowing you to respond to what you are reading with full comprehension).

Vision

In the case of vision, there are two kinds of receptors known as *rods* and *cones* (see the illustration overleaf). The 120 million rods and the 6 million cones are located in the retina of the eye. The rods are most densely present in the outer part of the retina, whereas the cones are mostly located in the central part of the retina; in the most central area—the fovea—there are only cones. Rods and cones efficiently perform two of the major tasks that we require of our visual system. Rods are extremely sensitive to light, and are approximately 500 times more sensitive to light than cones.

The sensitivity of rods means that movement in the periphery of vision can be detected very readily. Rods, however, are colour blind. In contrast, cones provide us with colour vision and help us to make fine discriminations. Colour vision is possible because there are three types of cone, each possessing different photopigments. One type of cone is maximally sensitive to light from the short-wavelength area of the spectrum; a second type responds most to medium-wavelength light; and the third type responds maximally to long-wavelength light. Perceived colour, however, is not affected only by the wavelength of the light reflected from an object. For example, when the cones have been stimulated by a bright stimulus for some time, *negative afterimages* will appear in the colour that is complementary to that of the original stimulus (e.g., blue and reddish-yellow are complementary colours, and so are red and bluish-green). These afterimages are due to a combination of photopigment bleaching (which reduces the sensitivity of the cones to the wavelengths to which they have just been exposed) and neural rebound (increased firing of some of the non-stimulated cones when the stimulus ceases).

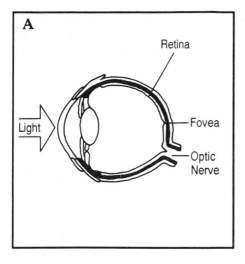

A

Retina

Light

Fovea

Optic
Nerve

Box A contains a simplified diagram of a cross section of the eye. Box B shows a diagram of simplified rods and cones. Information collected by the sensory membranes at the ends of the rods and cones is transmitted to the optic nerve by a network of neurones. Box C illustrates how an object in the right visual field is received on the left side of the brain via the optic chiasma, and vice versa.

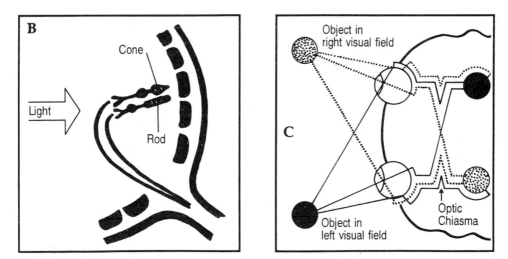

B

Cone

Light

Rod

C

Object in
right visual field

Object in
left visual field

Optic
Chiasma

As shown in the illustration, information from the visual receptors passes along the optic nerve to the optic chiasma. The optic nerves from each eye converge on the optic chiasma, where something rather strange happens. Information from that half of each retina which is nearer to the nose crosses over to the other side of the brain, but information from the half of each retina further from the nose does not. Each of the optic tracts beyond the optic chiasma thus carries some information from both eyes. Axons (long appendages of nerve cells) in the optic tract synapse in the lateral geniculate nucleus carry information to Area 17 in the occipital lobe of the cortex. For the sake of completeness, it should be noted that there are further visual processing regions in Areas 18 and 19 of the occipital lobe, and that there are also visual pathways to sub-cortical centres (i.e. centres below the level of the cortex).

The single cell recording technique. A major breakthrough in our understanding of the physiology of the visual cortex was made a number of years ago by David Hubel and Torsten Wiesel (1962). They pioneered the use of the single cell recording technique. This involves inserting a microelectrode into some part of the visual system, and then amplifying the tiny electrical changes produced by external visual stimulation and displaying them on the screen of an *oscilloscope*. Careful use of this technique with cats and monkeys allowed them to identify three different kinds of cell in the brain's visual system:

- *Simple cells* in Area 17 show maximal response to lines having a specific orientation in a specific part of the retina.
- *Complex cells* in Area 18 resemble simple cells, except that the point where the line is on the retina is much less important.
- Finally, there are *hypercomplex cells* in Area 19, which differ from complex cells mainly because they respond maximally to lines of a specific length.

One of the reasons why the discoveries of Hubel and Wiesel are so important is that they appear to provide tangible evidence of some of the basic components of the brain's visual system involved in form perception. However, Hubel and Wiesel were not correct in every respect. They argued that the three kinds of cell were hierarchically arranged, with the output of simple cells forming complex cells, and with complex cells terminating at hypercomplex cells. It is now generally agreed that matters are actually more complicated. The fact that complex cells sometimes respond faster than simple cells to stimulation indicates that at least some complex cells do not consist of simple cells; instead, complex cells seem to be connected directly to the lateral geniculate nucleus.

The cells in the visual cortex discovered by Hubel and Wiesel seem to be more adaptable than was thought at one time. Consider, for example, a study carried out by Colin Blakemore, who reared cats in the dark (see Blakemore, 1975). Their cortical cells were modified by exposure to a vertically striped cylinder for one hour, with most of the cells becoming selectively responsive to vertical lines. Thus, environmental factors can have a signficant impact on these cortical cells, which may be extremely useful when coping with unusual surroundings.

Hearing

The auditory system is reasonably complex, and only the flavour of what is involved can be given here. In the first place, sound waves travel from the *tympanic membrane* (the eardrum) to three bones known as the *ossicles* (see the diagram below). From the ossicles, information passes to the *fenestra ovalis*, which is an opening in the bone that surrounds the inner ear. From there, information passes to the *cochlea*, which is a coiled tube filled with liquid. There are two cochleas, one on each side of the head. Inside each cochlea there are hair cells between two membranes (pliable sheet-like tissues), and sound waves cause the membranes to move and thus affect the hair cells. This in turn produces action potentials in the auditory nerve. Information from each cochlea passes to both sides of the brain, as well as to sub-cortical areas.

The most straightforward dimension of auditory stimulation is loudness, which relates to the intensity of auditory experience. Loudness

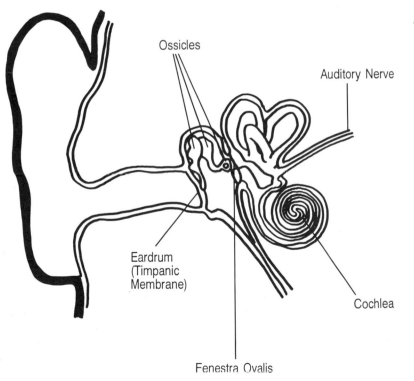

A simplified diagram of the human ear, showing some of the major structures.

Ossicles

Auditory Nerve

Eardrum
(Timpanic
Membrane)

Cochlea

Fenestra Ovalis

depends essentially on the amplitude of vibration of the sound wave, which determines the number of neurons that are firing in the auditory nerve. Another dimension is pitch. The major determinant of pitch is the frequency of vibration of the sound wave, with higher pitch being produced by higher frequencies. Pitch, however, is affected by the intensity of the auditory stimulus as well as by its frequency. Increased intensity leads to increased pitch for tones with frequencies above approximately 3000 Hz, but it produces decreased pitch for tones below 100 Hz.

Sensory thresholds

In all of the sense modalities, attempts have been made to distinguish two kinds of sensory threshold: the *absolute threshold* and the *differential threshold*. The absolute threshold is the least intense stimulus that is detectable, whereas the differential threshold is the smallest change in the stimulus that can be detected. In the last century, Gustav Fechner discovered that it is impossible to establish precise values for these thresholds, because they seem to fluctuate over time. Nevertheless, it is probably better to abandon the notion of fixed absolute and differential thresholds altogether, as has been done in *signal-detection theory*. According to this theory, there is continuously fluctuating activity (called "noise") in the sensory system, even in the absence of any stimulus. The subject's task in an absolute threshold experiment is to decide whether the activity in the sensory system is due solely to noise, or whether it is due to noise plus a stimulus. The difficulty of making this decision varies from moment to moment as a function of the amount of spontaneous activity or noise. It is therefore meaningless to think in terms of fixed thresholds.

Signal-detection theory also states that account has to be taken of how cautious people are when deciding to say that they have detected a stimulus or a change in a stimulus. It provides separate measures of sensitivity and of response cautiousness. Someone who indicates detection on the basis of very modest evidence may appear to have lower thresholds than someone who is more cautious. The same person will give far more false alarms—i.e. saying that a stimulus was there when it was not. So in order to reach an accurate assessment of the person's true sensitivity to the presence of a stimulus or to a change in a stimulus, you have to take account of his or her degree of cautiousness in responding.

Psychophysical functions

Gustav Fechner (1860) introduced the term *psychophysics* to refer to an area of research concerned with the relationships between stimuli and the resultant sensations. He hoped to be able to state in precise mathematical terms the rules of translation between the mental and physical realms. As we saw in the previous section, an investigation of absolute and differential thresholds was one of the aspects of psychophysics in which Fechner was interested. While he was not entirely successful in bridging the gap between the mental and the physical, it is nevertheless true that some of the earliest properly scientific research in psychology emerged in the area of psychophysics.

What we will consider here is the relationship between the *actual* energy level or intensity of the presented stimulus on the one hand, and the *perceived* intensity of sensation on the other hand. This issue has been looked at in connection with several different sense modalities and using various different ways of measuring the intensity of sensations. A very simple technique known as *magnitude estimation* was advocated by Stevens (1951). The subjects simply assign numbers to stimuli in relation to the apparent magnitudes of the sensations produced. Thus, if one tone sounds twice as loud or intense as another, or one light looks twice as bright as another, the subject simply assigns a number which is double that given to the other stimulus. Quite unusually for psychology, it turns out that there is a simple way of accounting for the data—the power law of sensory perception (see panel).

Stevens's power law of sensory intensity

The relationship between stimulus and sensation for virtually all sensory attributes that are quantitative in nature can be described reasonably accurately by Stevens's (1951) power law of sensory intensity. This law states that the subjective intensity of a stimulus is proportional to its physical intensity raised to some power. In simpler terms, the law states that equal ratios of stimulus intensity produce equal ratios of sensation intensity. For example, two sounds with a ratio of 8:1 in stimulus intensity produce sensations of loudness with a ratio of 2:1. This means that to double the perceived loudness of almost any sound, it is necessary to increase the intensity of the sound approximately eight-fold.

The picture is rather different with electric shock, although Stevens's power law still applies. In order to double perceived electric shock, the electrical energy of any shock must be multiplied by approximately 1.6. What all this means is that, armed only with a single figure representing the relationship between the physical intensity ratio and the sensation ratio, we can readily predict the difference in subjective intensity of any two stimuli differing in their physical intensities.

Perceptual development

Innate versus learned

Philosophers over the centuries have speculated on the relative importance of innate or inborn factors and of learning in perception. One extreme position was adopted by the English philosopher John Locke. He claimed that the mind at birth is a *tabula rasa* (literally, a blank tablet). According to this view, perception is possible only after prolonged experience and learning. The opposite position was favoured in the early years of this century by many German psychologists belonging to the *Gestalt* school of psychology (discussed later in this chapter). They claimed that the crucial perceptual processes are innate and do not depend directly on experience. In between is a compromise position, supported by most psychologists, according to which innate factors and learned or environmental factors are both of vital significance in the development of perception.

One way of investigating this theoretical issue is to study humans who have little or no relevant perceptual experience. If perception is innately determined, their perceptual processing should be adequate, but if perception depends on learning, it should be grossly deficient. You might think that new-born infants (or neonates as they are usually called) would be ideal subjects. There are, however, great problems in deciding what (if anything) they are perceiving, since they manifestly cannot describe their perceptual experience to us. There is, nevertheless, interesting evidence indicating that at least some perceptual skills do not require learning. For example, Michael Wertheimer (1962) presented a new-born baby less than ten minutes old with a series of sounds. Some of the sounds were to the baby's left and some were to his right. The baby looked in the appropriate direction every time, suggesting that primitive auditory processes are available at birth.

Neonates also appear to possess some basic visual processes. For example, Adams, Maurer, and Davis (1986) discovered that neonates could distinguish grey from colours such as green, yellow, and red. For each of these colours the neonates preferred colour and grey draughtboards to grey squares of the same brightness. In other words, some degree of colour vision and discrimination is present at birth.

The issue of whether perception is innate has also been looked at by studying adults who were blind at birth, but subsequently gained their sight (e.g. via the surgical removal of cataracts). Without exception, as von Senden (1932) discovered, such individuals have all found visual perception extremely difficult, and some have never progressed beyond basic

"WE WANT JUNIOR TO ASSOCIATE THE RINGING BELL WITH FEEDING TIME, BUT IT DOESN'T SEEM TO HAVE ANY EFFECT...."

perceptual skills. Although the implication of these findings is that visual perception is not innate or inborn, there are strong grounds for doubting such a conclusion. The individuals concerned had all spent several years developing special skills to compensate for their lack of vision, and these skills may have interfered with the learning of specifically visual skills. In addition, the sudden change from being blind to being sighted often produced emotional and motivational difficulties which may have restricted the development of visual perception.

A rather different research strategy involves the use of animals. It is possible to rear animals in darkness from birth—something that would be morally indefensible with human infants. Of course, many people argue that it is equally indefensible to conduct such research on animals—it is a matter of individual conscience and morality. When animals reared in darknesss are first exposed to light, their visual ability is considerably less than that of normally reared animals of the same age. This suggests that learning plays an important part in perceptual development, but the evidence cannot be accepted at face value. Post-mortem examinations have shown that those animals reared in darkness often have some degeneration of the retina and occasionally also of the optic nerve.

A better approach is to rear animals in diffuse, unpatterned light, which does not produce physiological degeneration. The usual finding is that these animals exhibit skills of visual perception which are inferior to those of normally reared animals, but superior to those of animals reared in darkness. They tend to experience problems in avoiding obstacles and also in making visual discriminations.

The question of the relative importance of innate factors and learning in perceptual development has not yet been resolved. It does appear probable, however, that innate factors and learning are both essential to normal perceptual development. It is also very likely that some perceptual processes are much more affected than others by experience and by learning. Some of the basic elements of perception (e.g. perception of movement; certain aspects of depth perception) seem to be either innate or else acquired very quickly. In contrast, fine perceptual discriminations among objects (e.g. the ability to distinguish visually between similar letters such as "b" and "d") may require much learning.

We can conclude that while innate factors provide some of the building blocks of perception, the complex perceptual processing of which adults are capable is learned over years of experience with the perceptual world. Some of these matters are dealt with further in the next section.

Perception in infants

The theoretical controversy of innate versus learned led a number of psychologists to make a thorough examination of perceptual development over the first few months of life. The prevalent view used to be that the perceptual experience of the infant was, in the words of William James, a "booming, buzzing confusion". It is now generally acknowledged that infants possess greater perceptual skills. Research carried out by Robert Fantz (1961) was important in changing the climate of opinion. He made use of a preference task in which a number of visual stimuli were presented at the same time. If an infant consistently tended to look at one stimulus for longer than the others, this selectivity was thought to demonstrate the existence of perceptual discrimination.

Examples of the stimuli used by Fantz.

Let us have a closer look at the preference task by considering a classic study by Fantz (1961). He showed infants (between the ages of four days and five months) head-shaped discs resembling those shown on page 20. Infants of all ages looked most at the realistic face and least at the blank face. On the basis of this, and other similar studies, Fantz (1966) arrived at the following sweeping conclusions:

> The findings have tended to destroy … myths—that the world of the neonate is a big booming confusion, that his visual field is a form of blur, that his mind is a blank slate, that his brain is decorticate, and that his behaviour is limited to reflexes or undirected mass movements. The infant sees a patterned and organised world which he explores discriminatingly within the limited means at his command. [pp. 171–172].

Findings from the preference task do not really warrant these conclusions. At an experimental level, the difference in time spent looking at the real and the scrambled faces was relatively modest in the study by Fantz (1961), and other researchers have sometimes been unable to find any difference. At an interpretative level, it is entirely possible that infants look at the real face not because it is a face but simply because it is a complex, symmetrical visual stimulus.

The visual cliff.   Eleanor Gibson and Richard Walk (1960) also argued that infants possess well-developed perceptual skills. They designed a "visual cliff", which was actually a glass-top table. A check pattern was positioned close to the glass under one half of the table (the "shallow" side) and far below the glass under the other half (the "deep" side)—see the diagram. Infants between the ages of 6½ and 12 months were placed on the shallow side of the table, and encouraged to crawl over the edge of the

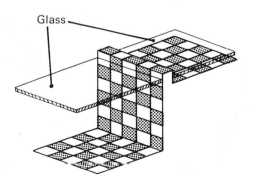

Glass

A diagram of the "visual cliff" set-up.

visual cliff on to the deep side by being offered toys or having their mothers call them. A majority of the infants failed to respond to these incentives, presumably because they possessed at least some of the elements of depth perception.

This work on the visual cliff does not necessarily indicate that depth perception is innate, because infants who are several months old might have learned about depth perception from experience. There is some intriguing physiological evidence pointing to the importance of learning in the visual cliff situation. Nine-month-old infants had faster heart rates than normal when placed on the deep side, presumably because they were frightened. Younger infants of two months, on the other hand, actually had *slower* heart rates than usual when placed on the deep side, suggesting that they did not perceive depth, and so were unafraid. This slowing of heart rate probably reflected interest on the part of the infants, and it certainly indicates that they detected some difference between the deep and shallow sides of the visual cliff situation.

Other evidence.   More convincing evidence that infants have at least the rudiments of depth perception was obtained by Bower, Broughton, and Moore (1970). They showed two objects to infants under two weeks old. One was large and approached to within 20 centimetres of the infant's face, whereas the other was small and approached to eight centimetres. The objects had the same retinal size (i.e. size at the retina) at their closest point to the infant. In spite of this, the infants were more disturbed by the object which came closer to them. Apparently these infants somehow made use of information about depth to identify which object posed the greater threat.

An important characteristic of adult perception is the existence of various kinds of *constancy* (e.g. size, shape). That is to say, we perceive a given object as having the same size and shape regardless of its distance from us or its orientation. In other words, we see things "as they really are", and are not fooled by variations in the information presented to the retina. This is more of an achievement than might be supposed, because the retinal image of an object is very much smaller when the object is a long way away from us than when it is very close. Thomas Bower has addressed the issue of whether infants demonstrate these constancies. In one study (Bower, 1964), for example, he examined size constancy in infants between 75 and 85 days old. The first stage of the experiment involved teaching the infants to look at a 30-centimetre cube placed approximately one metre from them. As illustrated in the diagram overleaf, Bower then compared the length of time spent looking at the same cube placed 3 metres from the infant and a 90-centimetre cube placed 3 metres away. The former stimulus

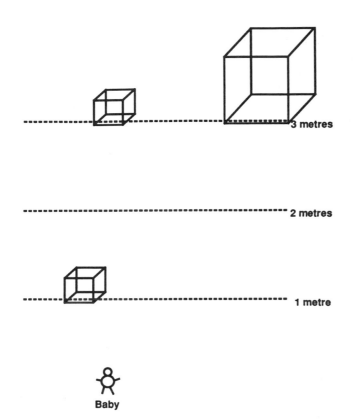

3 metres

2 metres

1 metre

Baby

had the same real size as the original cube, of course, but a much smaller retinal image, whereas the latter stimulus had a considerably greater real size but the same retinal size as the original cube. Some size constancy was demonstrated by the fact that the infants were almost three times likelier to look at the former than at the latter stimulus object. However, the infants failed to show complete size constancy, because they were more likely to look at the 30-centimetre cube when it was placed one metre away rather than three metres away.

Bower has obtained very similar results from his studies of shape constancy. In essence, infants as young as two months show some evidence of shape constancy, but the level of constancy exhibited is less than that of adults. The conclusion to which one is drawn is that very young infants have surprisingly well-developed perceptual processes. Are these perceptual skills innately determined? Since Bower was studying infants who were two or three months of age, it is obviously possible that they may have learned at least some of the perceptual skills involved. However, it is worth noting that the exploratory and reaching activities that might lead to the learning of relevant perceptual skills do not usually begin until infants are at least three months of age.

We have focused so far on the perceptual achievements of infants. They also display perceptual deficiencies. While they are very good at locating objects within the visual field, they are not able to process visual information in the systematic and precise way that adults can. For example, if infants are shown a complex visual object, they tend to fixate on just part of it rather than exploring all of its major features.

Very young infants thus possess more of the basic mechanisms of perception than might have been anticipated. According to Alan Slater (1990), an expert in the field:

> No modality [none of the senses] operates at adult-like levels at birth, but such levels are achieved suprisingly early in infancy, leading to recent conceptualisations of the "competent infant". ... A reasonable view is that early perceptual competence is matched by cognitive incompetence, and that much of the reorganisation of perceptual representation is dependent upon the development and construction of cognitive structures that give access to a world of objects, people, language, and events. [p. 262].

Perceptual processes after infancy

In general terms, there is a fairly steady improvement in perceptual processes in the childhood years following infancy. For example, the partial shape constancy exhibited by infants improves to an adult level of performance by about the age of 14. A similar pattern is found with distance perception. If a child stands at one end of a corridor, and is asked to indicate a point halfway down the corridor, the point chosen will usually be too near to the child. In other words, the further part of the corridor is misjudged as being shorter than it actually is. Performance on this task steadily improves throughout the childhood years.

The problem experienced by younger children with distance perception is relevant to another interesting finding. Children are typically as accurate as adults in their assessments of the sizes of objects that are reasonably close to them, but their performance is often very inaccurate when judging the sizes of distant objects. Even in adults there are residues of this problem. For example, when you look out of the window of a plane it is hard to believe that the tiny dots below you are actually quite large houses.

One of the most important studies on perceptual development in children was reported by Eleanor Gibson (1969). She asked children aged between four and eight to select from thirteen figures the only one that was identical to a standard stimulus figure. The other 12 figures differed slightly from the standard figure in various ways. Some differed in orientation (i.e. the figure was rotated or inverted), and others differed in perspective (i.e. the figure was made to appear slanted or tilted backwards). Not surprisingly, the number of errors decreased with age. More interestingly, the pattern of errors changed with age. Perspective errors were very common at all ages, whereas orientation errors were very frequent among the four-year-olds but almost non-existent among the eight-year-olds.

A plausible interpretation of these results is that they reflect the acquisition of the skills involved in reading and writing. The orientation of the stimulus is not important when a child is looking at a toy from different angles, but in reading and writing it is crucial for differentiating letters (e.g. the letters b, d, p, and q differ primarily in orientation). In contrast, perspective changes are of little consequence whether children are trying to identify objects or letters.

How should we regard the process of perceptual development in children? According to Eleanor and James Gibson, the major process is one of *perceptual differentiation*. They argued that the stimuli presented to our sense organs contain all the information we need for accurate perception. What happens during the course of perceptual development is that children gradually learn to identify the crucial features of any stimulus. Thus, in the study by Eleanor Gibson which we have just discussed, older children were much better able than younger ones to make use of the stimulus feature of orientation.

A very different view of perceptual development is the *perceptual enrichment hypothesis*. According to this hypothesis, the stimuli presented to our senses are often rather impoverished in terms of the information they provide. Accurate perception develops as children learn to supplement sensory information with their increasing body of relevant knowledge and experience. For example, someone who plays tennis a lot can tell simply from the sound of the racquet hitting the ball whether or not the ball has been hit cleanly.

It is entirely possible, of course, that perceptual development involves both differentiation and enrichment. Which process is used presumably depends on the quality of the stimulus information. Complex visual stimuli presented for a long period of time in bright light require perceptual differentiation for accurate perception, whereas visual stimuli presented very briefly in dim light need perceptual enrichment.

Perceptual organisation

One of the most striking characteristics of perception is the fact that it is nearly always highly organised. Our visual world consists of objects arranged meaningfully in three-dimensional space, and this happens so naturally and effortlessly that it is hard to believe that organised perception is actually a substantial achievement. The fact that computers can be programmed to play high-level chess, but cannot as yet be programmed to match the visual skills of even relatively primitive animals supports this idea.

The information that arrives at the sense receptors is confusing and disorganised. In the case of vision, there is usually a mosaic of colours, and the retinal sizes and shapes of objects in the environment may correspond very poorly to their actual sizes and shapes. We look at the factors involved in making sense of our sensations, and turning them into organised perception is the subject matter of the following sections.

Form perception and the Gestaltists

One of the most fundamental characteristics of perceptual organisation is the way in which the visual field is segregated into one or more objects that are the central focus—the so-called "figure"—and everything else, which forms the "ground". The figure is typically closer to the perceiver than is the ground, and is processed more thoroughly.

German psychologists in the early twentieth century who were interested in the figure–ground phenomenon called the figure in a visual display the "Gestalt", which is a German word meaning "organised whole", and led to them becoming known as the Gestaltists. They proposed numerous laws of perceptual organisation, but their most basic principle was the *law of Pragnanz*, which is as follows (Kurt Koffka, 1935): "Psychological organisation will always be as 'good' as the prevailing conditions allow. In this definition the term 'good' is undefined" [p. 110]. Koffka was unnecessarily vague in his second sentence, since a good form was usually regarded by the Gestaltists as being the most simple or uniform of the potential organizational structures.

The Gestaltist approach can be seen most clearly if we consider some concrete examples (set out in the figure overleaf). Pattern (a) is most naturally seen as three horizontal arrays of dots. This illustrates the Gestalt law of proximity, according to which visual elements which are close to each other will tend to be grouped together. In pattern (b), vertical columns rather than horizontal rows are seen. This accords with the law of similarity, according to which similar visual elements are grouped together. In pattern (c), we tend to see two crossing lines rather than a V-shaped line

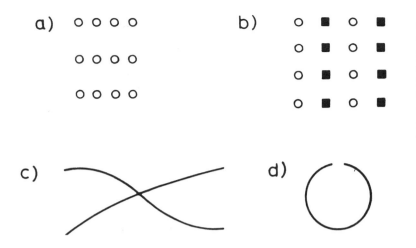

Examples of some of the Gestalt laws of perceptual organisation: a) the law of proximity; b) the law of similarity; c) the law of good continuation; and d) the law of closure.

and an inverted V-shaped line. This follows from the law of good continuation, which states that those visual elements producing the fewest interruptions to smoothly curving lines are grouped together. Finally, pattern (d) demonstrates the law of closure—i.e. the missing parts of a figure are filled in to complete it. It is worth noting that all of the laws exemplified in the patterns in the figure can be regarded as more specific statements of the fundamental laws of Pragnanz.

Where do these organisational processes come from? The Gestaltists argued that most perceptual organisation reflects the basic and largely innately determined functioning of the perceptual system. This seems unlikely to be the whole story, however. Our everyday experiences teach us that those visual elements which are similar and close to each other usually belong to the same visual object, whereas visual elements which are dissimilar and far apart do not.

The Gestalt laws of organisation seem reasonable, but they have nevertheless attracted much criticism. The major weakness is that the laws are only descriptive statements: they fail to explain why it is that similar visual elements or those close together are grouped together. Another limitation is that most of the Gestalt laws relate primarily or exclusively to the perceived organisation of two-dimensional patterns. Other factors come into play with three-dimensional scenes. For example, it may only be possible to separate out the figure of a chameleon from its background when it moves. Finally, it is extremely difficult to apply the Gestalt laws of organisation to certain complex visual stimuli (e.g. stimuli in which similar elements are relatively far apart and dissimilar elements are close together).

One of the best known assumptions made by the Gestaltists is that "the whole is more than the sum of its parts". Exactly what they meant by this is a little obscure. However, one of the testable implications is that the overall Gestalt or whole may be perceived before the parts making up that Gestalt. This may sound like putting the cart before the horse, because it has usually been assumed that the individual parts or features of a visual stimulus are processed before the overall object is identified.

The Gestaltist theoretical position was put to the test in an important study by David Navon (1977). He presented his subjects with rather strange stimuli. One was a large letter H formed out of numerous little Ss, and another was a large letter S formed out of little Hs. In addition, there was a large letter H formed from little Hs, and a larger letter S formed from little Ss. The task was to identify either the single large letter or the small letters as rapidly as possible. The time taken to identify the large letter was not affected by whether the small letters were the same as the large letter or different. In contrast, the time taken to identify the small letters was much longer when the large letter differed from them than when it was the same. This happened because information about the whole (i.e. the identity of the large letter) was available before information about the parts (i.e. the identity of the small letters). Interference was produced when small letters had to be identified and their identity differed from that of the large letter.

An implication of Navon's work is that early perceptual processing identifies the most important objects within the visual scene. Subsequent perceptual processing then provides more fine-grained analysis of the detailed structure of those objects. It is unlikely, however, that perceptual processing always proceeds in this fashion. If the parts of a visual object are unusually large or prominent, then they may be analysed at a very early stage of perceptual processing (Kinchla & Wolf, 1979).

Spatial perception

When we look around us, we do not simply see various objects of different sizes, shapes, and colours. What we actually perceive is a three-dimensional space, within which some objects are fairly close to us and other objects are further away. We are able to decide accurately on the relative distances of different objects because the environment provides us with several useful cues to distance. For example, if one object partially obscures a second object, then the first object must be closer to us. Size can be another powerful cue. If an object is of known size, then the size of its retinal image will indicate its approximate distance. Other cues include the fact that objects which are a long way away appear less distinct than objects which are close, and that objects which are further away generally appear higher in the visual field than those which are closer.

The Ames room.   A dramatic demonstration of the power of some of these cues is provided by the Ames room shown in the photograph. This is a specially constructed distorted room of a most peculiar shape: the floor slopes and the rear wall is not at right angles to the adjoining walls. Despite these peculiarities, the room stimulates the same retinal image as a normal rectangular room when viewed from a point in the front wall. The fact that one end of the rear wall is considerably further from the viewer than the other end is disguised by making it much higher. The cues misleadingly indicating that the rear wall is at right angles to the viewer are so strong that a person walking backwards and forwards immediately in front of the rear wall appears to grow and shrink as he or she advances!

Our ability to see the visual world "in depth" is enhanced by the fact that we have binocular—i.e. two-eyed—vision. It should be noted at the outset, however, that the various advantages of binocular over monocular (one-eyed) vision are much greater at relatively short distances up to a few metres, and are of little or no value at long distances. One of the binocular cues to depth is given by *convergence,* which involves both eyes fixating on the same object. The eyes need to turn inwards more if the object is close by than if it is some distance away, and so the extent of this turning inwards is a cue to distance. Another cue to distance is provided by *binocular*

The Ames Room.
Photograph copyright
© Eastern County
Newspapers Ltd.,
Norwich. Used by
permission.

disparity, which refers to the fact that the two eyes receive slightly different views of the world because of their different locations in the head.

The discrepancy in the information presented to each retina will be much more marked in the case of very close objects than far distant ones. The importance of binocular disparity was shown 150 years ago by Charles Wheatstone. He invented the stereoscope, which takes two pictures of the same scene from slightly different perspectives, simulating the perspectives of the eyes. When one picture is presented to each eye simultaneously under appropriate conditions, the viewer sees the scene three-dimensionally.

We have so far discussed spatial perception involving a stationary viewer looking at a static visual scene. In everyday life, of course, additional information about the distance of objects from us is provided by our own movements. As we move towards an object, its retinal size will increase much more rapidly if it is close to us than if it is a long way away. Another cue is provided by *motion parallax*, which is based on the relative movements of objects which are at different distances from the viewer. The next time you travel by train, look out of the window and focus on an object about half-way to the horizon. You should find that everything lying further away than the point of fixation appears to be travelling in the same direction that you are, while everything in front of the fixated object appears to be travelling in the opposite direction.

There is a wealth of different kinds of information that we use to provide ourselves with an accurate three-dimensional perceptual field, with the objects within it arranged at different distances from us. We have discussed several of the cues here, but we do not have the space to deal with all of them.

Constancies and illusions

As we discussed earlier in this chapter, perceptual constancies (e.g. size, shape) involve seeing visual objects accurately, regardless of their distance away from us or other factors that can distort or alter the retinal image. Thus, for example, the clock on the wall appears to have a round face, despite the fact that its shape in the retinal image is probably an ellipse. In the case of size constancy, it is reasonably certain that we use information about the distance an object is from us in order to assess its size accurately. If the viewing conditions are arranged so that most of the cues to the distance of an object are absent (e.g. monocular viewing in dim light with no other objects in view), then judgements of object size become inaccurate and there is little evidence of size constancy.

Since the apparent distance of an object is used to estimate its size, it follows that a mistake in the judgement of distance will tend to produce an error in the judgement of size. According to the English psychologist, Richard Gregory, and other perception theorists, exactly this kind of mistake is involved in many of the well-known perceptual illusions. Nature provides one of the most intriguing of such effects in the moon illusion. The moon when overhead appears to be much smaller than when it is close to the horizon. While there is no simple explanation of this illusion, one relevant factor seems to be that the sky at the horizon appears to be further away than the sky overhead. If the moon (whose retinal image remains the same) appears to be further away in some sense when it is close to the horizon, then we conclude that it must be larger.

Gregory's misapplied size-constancy theory. Richard Gregory (1970) put forward a *misapplied size-constancy theory,* according to which the processes that produce size constancy with three-dimensional objects are sometimes applied inappropriately to the perception of two-dimensional objects. Consider the best known visual illusion of all, the Müller-Lyer illusion, shown alongside. The vertical lines in the two figures are actually the same length, but the one in the figure on the left appears longer than the one in the figure on the right. Gregory used his misapplied size-constancy theory to explain this illusion in the following way. The Müller-Lyer figures can be thought of as simple perspective drawings of three-dimensional objects. The left figure resembles the inside corners of a room, whereas the right figure is like the outside corner of a building. Thus, the vertical line in the left figure is in some sense further away from us than its fins, whereas the vertical line in the right figure is closer to us than its fins. Since the size of the retinal image is the same for both vertical lines, the principle of size constancy tells us that the line which is further away (i.e. the one in the left figure) must be longer. This is precisely the Müller-Lyer illusion.

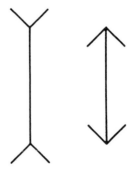

Gregory's theory has been applied in a very similar fashion to several other visual illusions. Support for the theory comes from the finding that the two-dimensional Müller-Lyer figures do indeed appear three-dimensional when they are presented as luminous models in a dark room. Gregory argues that it is only when these (and other) figures are presented on a flat surface that we do not perceive them as three-dimensional objects.

Despite the ingenuity of Gregory's theory, and the experimental support it has received, it does not provide a complete account of the visual illusions. The Müller-Lyer illusion can still be obtained when the fins on the two figures are replaced by squares or circles, and it is not at all clear how this could be attributed to misapplied size constancy. It is more plausible to assume that the apparent lengths of the vertical lines in this case are affected by whether they are part of a large or a small object. The fairest conclusion is probably that misapplied size constancy is the major factor producing visual illusion effects, but it is by no means the only one.

Perception of movement

One of the key characteristics of vision is the perception of movement. There are various sources of information which tell us that an individual or object is moving. For example, objects that are moving typically do so against a stationary background. Movement can be inferred from the changing position of the object relative to its background. Strictly speaking, this does not provide unambiguous evidence that the object itself has moved, because it is possible (although often improbable) that the background has moved rather than the object. One rather striking illusory effect which illustrates how information about relative changes of position can be misinterpreted springs to mind. The author's son, Willie, was gazing upwards at the folly in the grounds of Chatsworth, and there were clouds moving quickly by in the background. In some consternation he said, "Look, Dad, the tower's falling down!", and, indeed, the relative movement of the tower against the clouds did create that impression. This phenomenon is known as *induced movement*, because apparent movement of the object in question is brought about by movement of surrounding objects.

Another major source of information about movement comes from *image displacement*, which involves position shifts of the image of a stimulus on the retina. This happens when something moves across our field of vision, but we do not follow it with our eyes. There are probably cells in the human visual system which are selectively sensitive to movement in specific directions. This is suggested by a phenomenon known as the *movement after-effect*. For example, if you gaze at a waterfall for a minute or so, and then look away at other objects, such as a group of trees, these objects will appear to float upwards. This illusory movement in the opposite direction to previously seen real movement constitutes the movement after-effect. It is usually assumed that the cells sensitive to downward movement respond so much to the waterfall that they lose their sensitivity for a short time afterwards. As a result, the detectors sensitive to upward movement are more active than those sensitive to downward movement, and illusory upward movement is seen.

There is a further kind of information that influences the perception of movement. Sometimes when an object (e.g. a bird or a plane) moves rapidly in front of our field of vision, we track it with our eyes in such a way that its image remains in very much the same area of the retina. This is known as *ocular pursuit*. The usefulness of the information provided by ocular pursuit can be seen if a light is moved about within an otherwise completely dark room. An observer who tracks the light nearly always reports that it is moving, despite the absence of any cues to movement other than those provided by ocular pursuit.

Pattern recognition

One of the most crucial functions of visual perception is to assign meaning to the objects in the visual field by recognising or identifying them. This process of pattern recognition typically seems to require no effort on our part except under very rare circumstances (e.g. trying to drive in thick fog). It is extremely difficult, however, to account for pattern recognition. How is it, for example, that we can recognise the letter "A" across enormous variations in typeface, size, orientation, and writing style?

At a very general and abstract level, pattern recognition clearly depends on matching information from the visual stimulus with information stored in long-term memory. As a result of this matching process, the observer makes a decision as to the most likely identity of the visual stimulus.

One theoretical approach assumes that information about the visual stimulus is matched against miniature copies (usually called *templates*) of previously presented patterns which are stored in long-term memory. Whichever template produces the closest match to the stimulus input determines the outcome of the pattern-recognition process. How can template theories explain the fact that a pattern (for example a letter of the alphabet presented upside down) can be recognised easily even if its shape, size, and orientation are all rather unusual? One proposed solution is that we possess separate templates for every possible instance of a pattern. The problems involved in storing such a vast amount of information, however, would seem to cast doubt on this theory.

A more plausible notion is to assume that the visual stimulus undergoes a normalisation process before the search for a matching template takes place. Normalisation involves transforming the visual stimulus to produce an internal representation of a standard position and size, thereby reducing the number of templates that need to be stored. However, achieving normalisation would usually be rather complicated, since it requires some processing system to recognise the correct size and orientation of each visual stimulus.

Template theories are therefore rather inadequate in accounting for pattern recognition. Their limitations are especially obvious when we consider visual stimuli belonging to categories such as books or buildings. It stretches credibility to imagine that a single template could represent all books or all buildings, and the same objection applies to many other wide ranging categories.

An alternative to template theories of pattern recognition is provided by *prototype theories*. In essence, prototype theories claim that every visual stimulus is a member of a class or category of stimuli, and as a result shares significant attributes of that category. The process of pattern recognition involves matching stimulus inputs against prototypes, which are abstract representations made up of the key attributes of a concept. For example, the prototype of a plane might consist of a long tube with two wings attached to it.

A major advantage of prototype theories over template theories is that the information which needs to be stored in long-term memory consists of a reasonable number of prototypes rather than an essentially infinite number of templates. There are, however, two disadvantages to prototype theories. First, they tend to be rather vague about the way in which the stimulus input is matched up with its appropriate prototype. Second, no account is taken of the fact that pattern recognition is often facilitated by the context in which a stimulus is seen (e.g. it is easier to recognise that a small white object is a golf ball if you are on a golf course rather than in a park). The effects of context on pattern recognition are usually not dealt with by prototype theories.

Feature theories of pattern recognition have also been proposed. They differ from prototype theories in that the emphasis is on the individual and separate elements of the stimulus rather than on the stimulus as a whole. According to feature theories, pattern recognition starts by extracting the features or distinctive parts from the stimulus that has just been presented. Thus, for example, one might argue that the main features of the letter "A" are two straight lines which meet or nearly meet and which have an angle of about 45 degrees between them, together with a cross-bar which intersects both of them.

This approach is promising, because stimuli differing substantially in size and orientation may nevertheless possess the same features, and thus be recognisable as belonging to the same category. Gibson, Shapiro, and Yonas (1968) applied a feature approach to the task of identifying letters of the alphabet. They argued that 12 different features were involved, such as horizontal line segments, vertical line segments, and closed loops, and that any letter of the alphabet could be identified correctly on the basis of which of these features it contained. According to this theory, when letters are presented so rapidly that they are sometimes wrongly identified, the mistakes will reflect the feature similarity between the letter actually presented and the incorrect guess. Thus, for example, "P" would be confused with "R", because they have a number of features in common, but "P" should not be confused with "C", because they do not. There is some experimental support for this prediction, but the evidence in general is not very convincing. It seems probable that feature theories do describe reasonably accurately some of the processes involved in pattern recognition.

Such theories are limited, however. Their emphasis is on bottom-up or stimulus-driven processing, but pattern recognition is also affected by top-down or conceptually-driven processing. Let us return to the issue of how we identify letters of the alphabet. It is well known that proof-reading is a difficult task, because while reading we tend to see what we expect to see (because of top-down processing). In a sense, errors in proof-reading occur because the evidence from feature analyses of the letters can be outweighed by our expectations of what will be presented.

Pattern recognition is clearly a complex process that typically involves a mixture of bottom-up and top-down processes. It seems probable that an analysis of the features of the stimulus input is one of the major bottom-up processes involved in pattern recognition, but this is not the whole story. Our general knowledge and the context in which stimuli are presented both play a part in determining the outcome of the pattern-recognition process.

Theories of perception

Gibson's direct perception theory

There are two main sources of information that can be used in perception. The first is the sensory information provided by external stimuli impinging on the sense organs. The second is the stored knowledge about the world which we can use to make plausible hypotheses about our environment. While most psychologists would argue that both sources of information are typically used in most perceptual situations, a more challenging approach was taken by James Gibson (1979). He argued that sensory information is much more useful than it is usually given credit for, so that complex hypothesis testing is rarely required.

We can illustrate Gibson's theoretical approach by considering the perception of slant or depth in visual perception. According to Gibson, the texture of the visual stimulus can provide very useful information. An object that slants will have increasing texture density as you look from its near edge to its far edge. If you were unwise enough to stand between the rails of a railway track, the details would become less clear as you looked into the distance along the track.

In fact, Gibson's interest in perceptual phenomena started during the Second World War, when he was given the task of preparing training films which would describe the problems that

pilots experience when landing. He discovered that *optic flow patterns* are experienced by a pilot when approaching a landing strip. What is experienced in these patterns is that the point towards which the pilot is moving appears motionless, with the rest of the visual environment apparently moving away from that point. The further any part of the landing strip is from that point, the greater is its apparent speed of movement. According to Gibson, the sensory information available to pilots in optic flow patterns provides pilots with unambiguous information about their direction, speed, and altitude.

We can perhaps accept Gibson's argument that the visual environment is usually a rich source of valuable information about the spatial layout of objects. However, it is a rather different matter to account for pattern recogniton and the way in which we manage to assign meaning to objects. The conventional view (discussed above) is that we attach meaning to stimuli by relating them in some fashion to our stored knowledge. Gibson rejected this view, and claimed that what actually happens is that the various possible uses of objects (which he called their *affordances*) are perceived directly. For example, one of the affordances of a chair is the fact that we can sit on it, and this quality of being capable of being sat on is allegedly contained within the sensory information that is provided by the stimulus of a chair.

Gibson's theory offers a reasonable explanation for the fact that perception is usually accurate. However, his theory is less adequate when accounting for the various errors and illusions that occur in perception. If it is true that sensory information is typically very rich and detailed, it is puzzling that we make so many perceptual errors. Apart from the visual illusions discussed earlier in this chapter, there is a general tendency for people to over-estimate vertical extents relative to horizontal ones (see the figure alongside in which the two lines are the same length). The vertical-horizontal illusion occurs in everyday life, as you can demonstrate with a cup, a saucer, and two spoons of the same length. If you put one spoon vertically in the cup and the other spoon horizontally in the saucer, you will find that the vertical spoon looks much longer than the horizontal one. Here we have apparently rich sensory information, and yet perception is mysteriously in error.

Constructive theories and a synthesis

Several perception theorists, among them Richard Gregory (1972) and Jerome Bruner (1957), have regarded the process of perception in a markedly different way from Gibson. According to them, perception is by no means determined entirely by the stimulus information presented to the senses; instead, perception is an active and constructive process which makes much use of top-down processes. The flavour of this theoretical approach is captured in the following quotation from Gregory (1972), who argued that perceptual experiences are constructions "from floating scraps of data signalled by the senses and drawn from the brain memory banks, themselves constructions from snippets of the past." Constructive theories of perception are supported in a general way by the finding that perception is sometimes inaccurate. Such inaccuracies are attributed to the fact that inadequate stimulus information will often be consistent with the wrong construction. However, if perception really involves educated guesses about the meaning of "scraps of data", then it is surprising that perception is usually rather accurate.

The solution seems to be some sort of synthesis of the Gibsonian and constructive approaches. One such synthesis was provided by Ulric Neisser (1976). As the diagram below illustrates, Neisser proposed that there is a perceptual cycle involving schemata (collections of knowledge derived from past experience), perceptual exploration, and the stimulus environment. Schemata serve the function of directing perceptual exploration towards relevant environmental stimuli. Such exploration often involves movement around the environment. Perceptual exploration leads the perceiver to sample some of the available stimulus information. If that information fails to match information in the relevant schema, then the information in the schema is modified appropriately.

Neisser's emphasis on the importance of schemata is consistent with the views of constructivist theorists that top-down processes play a major role in perception. He also includes Gibson's emphasis on bottom-up processes in the notion that the sampling of available environmental

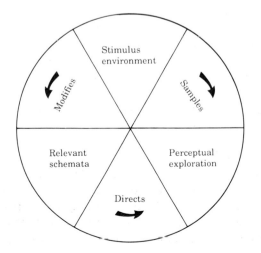

The perceptual cycle, as proposed by Neisser (1976).

information can modify the current schema. While Neisser's theoretical views are undeniably sketchy and lacking in detail, it is likely that they are on the right lines. There is one final important point which needs to be made, and which is consistent with Neisser's general theoretical position. It is likely that visual perception is primarily determined by sensory information and thus bottom-up processes when the viewing conditions are good, but that constructive top-down processes become more and more important as the viewing conditions deteriorate.

Computational theory

Theorising within perception has been increasingly influenced in recent years by the computer revolution. More specifically, attempts have been made to produce computer programs that will mimic some of the perceptual processes used by humans.

Marr's computational approach. The most celebrated computer-based approach is that of David Marr (1982). His computational approach to perception has as its starting point the assumption that it is important to distinguish between *what* perception accomplishes and *how* it is accomplished, which involves various mechanisms. Marr argued that in the case of visual perception it is important to understand what visual perception accomplishes before addressing the issue of the detailed mechanisms responsible for that accomplishment.

This computational approach led Marr (1982) to suggest that three visual representations of progressively greater complexity are formed during visual perception. The first representation is the *primal sketch*, which consists largely of information about features such as edges, contours, and blobs. The primal sketch is then used to facilitate the formation of a second representation, which is called the *2.5-D sketch*. This representation is more detailed than the primal sketch, and includes information about the depth and orientation of visible surfaces. It is not a complete representation, because it is observer-centred—i.e., the visual information is essentially retinal in nature. The third and final visual representation is the *3-D model representation*. This is free of the various limitations of the 2.5-D sketch. In particular, the 3-D sketch incorporates a three-dimensional representation which is independent of the observer's viewpoint, and it conforms to the visual constancies.

Some of the flavour of Marr's views on 3-D model representations can be obtained by considering the work of Marr and Nishihara (1978). They proposed that the basic units for describing objects are cylinders. They also proposed that these basic units are hierarchically organised, with high-level units providing information about object shape and low-level units

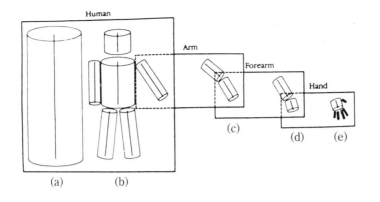

The hierarchical organisation of the human figure at different levels: a) axis of the whole body; b) axes at the level of arms, legs and head; c) arm divided into upper and lower arm; d) a lower arm with separate hand; and e) the palm and fingers of a hand. (Marr & Nishihara, 1978.)

providing more detailed information. The way in which the human form can be regarded as a series of cylinders at different levels of generality is shown in the diagram above.

It is difficult to convey the qualities of Marr's computational theory in a brief account, but let us consider a single example of his approach in action. It was mentioned earlier in the chapter that simple cells have been discovered which respond maximally to lines of a particular orientation. A number of theorists have used these findings to claim that these cells provide definitive evidence about line orientation. When Marr tried to produce a computer program to mimic the activity of these cells, however, he couldn't. The amount of activity in a specific simple cell proved too *ambiguous* to provide direct evidence of line orientation. For example, suppose there is a moderate level of activity in a simple cell which responds maximally to a horizontal line. This would occur when a rather faint horizontal line was presented, but it would also occur when a high-contrast line was presented just off the horizontal.

This example demonstrates the usefulness of combining information from the computational approach, from computer programming, and from neurophysiology. It also shows that basic perceptual processes can be considerably more complex than had generally been believed. An obvious limitation of the computational theory is that it focuses mainly on bottom-up processes, and has relatively little to say about the ways in which top-down processes based on prior experience with the visual environment affect the perceptual process. In addition, the fact that a computer program can be made to attain the same perceptual goals as human observers does not necessarily mean that the computer has arrived at those goals in precisely the same manner as the human.

Summary: Sensory systems and perception

- Physiologists can tell us something about the ways in which the information presented to our sense organs is transformed as it makes its way from the relevant sense organ to the central nervous system. Physiological evidence exposes some of the limitations of our sensory systems, which in turn set limits on our perceptual powers.
- The relationship between the intensity of the presented stimulus and the perceived intensity of sensation can usually be expressed in a relatively straightforward way by Stevens's power law of sensory intensity.
- One fundamental question is whether perception is innate or depends on learning experiences. Innate factors appear to provide some of the basic building blocks of perception, but complex perceptual processing and fine perceptual discriminations are possible only after years of perceptual experience. Perceptual development probably involves perceptual enrichment, in which children are increasingly able to supplement the information presented to the sense organs with relevant knowledge, and perceptual differentiation, in which children gradually learn to identify the crucial features of any stimulus.
- We usually create highly organised perception out of the confusing bombardment of stimulation to which we are normally exposed. One of the central tasks of perception theory is to explain how this happens. The Gestalt principles of laws of perceptual organisation are useful descriptions of what happens.
- Our ability to organise visual stimuli into perception of three-dimensional space depends on several cues, such as size, provided by the incoming stimulation. The processes involved in organised perception include: identification of cues provided by incoming stimuli; binocular vision; the study of visual illusion; and accurate perception of movement.
- Pattern recognition involves matching information from the visual stimulus with information stored in long-term memory.
- Many perception theorists have argued persuasively that perception depends on a combination of bottom-up or stimulus-driven processes and top-down or conceptually-driven processes. However, some theorists (e.g. Gibson) have argued that the stimulus generally contains so much relevant information that bottom-up processes are usually adequate to ensure accurate perception. In contrast, constructive theorists (e.g. Gregory) claim that perception is an active and constructive process which makes substantial use of top-down processes. It is probable (as argued by Neisser) that perception typically involves both bottom-up and top-down processes, with the latter processes becoming more important as the viewing conditions deteriorate.
- Marr's (1982) computational theory makes use of information from psychology and neurophysiology to produce computer programs designed to mimic certain aspects of human perceptual processing. This kind of multi-disciplinary approach to perception will probably become even more important in the future.

Further reading

One useful source of further reading is I. Roth and J. Frisby (1986), *Perception and Representation: A Cognitive Approach* (Milton Keynes: Open University Press), which deals with Marr's theory much more fully than we have been able to do here. Another source is M. W. Eysenck and M. T. Keane (1990), *Cognitive Psychology: A Student's Handbook* (Hove, U.K.: Lawrence Erlbaum Associates Ltd.), which covers most of the theoretical issues dealt with in this chapter.

3 Attention

The concept of attention has been used in so many senses that some psychologists feel it is altogether too vague and should be discarded. Sometimes it is a synonym for concentration, at other times it refers to our ability to select a piece of incoming stimulation for further analysis. Other psychologists have suggested that there are close links between attention and physiological arousal, with the aroused individual being more attentive to the environment than the drowsy one.

Perhaps it is most frequently used, however, to refer to selectivity of processing. The term was used in this sense by the great American psychologist, William James (1890), in the following quotation:

> Everyone knows what attention is. It is the taking possession by the mind, in clear and vivid form, of one out of what seem several simultaneously possible objects or trains of thought. Focalisation, concentration, of consciousness are of its essence. It implies withdrawal from some things in order to deal effectively with others [pp. 403-404].

Research designed to clarify how attention works makes an important distinction between *focused attention* and *divided attention*. Studies looking at focused attention ask people to process and respond to only one out of two or more stimuli presented at the same time. These studies enable us to investigate the processes involved in selective attention. Studies of divided attention ask people to attend to and process as best they can all the two or more stimuli presented together. The hope is that we will discover much of value about attentional mechanisms and their capacity.

Most of this chapter is devoted to analyses of focused and divided attention. The final section of the chapter, however, considers attention in terms of our ability to concentrate on or pay attention to tasks that are both monotonous and long-lasting. The term *vigilance* is generally used to refer to this area of interest.

Before going on to a more detailed discussion of attentional phenomena, it should be noted that there is a major limitation in most attentional

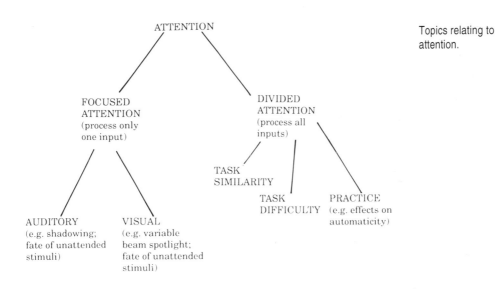

Topics relating to attention.

research. We all know that we can choose between attending to the *external* environment or to the *internal* environment (i.e. our own thoughts and information in long-term memory). Most of the work on attention, however, has been concerned with attention to the external environment. By far the most important reason for this is that experimenters can identify and control the stimuli presented in the external environment in a way that is simply not possible with internal determinants of attention.

The reader may find the diagram above useful as a point of reference throughout this chapter. It provides an indication of how some of the various topics within attention are related to each other. The structure of this chapter closely follows that indicated in the diagram.

Selective or focused attention

Nearly all of the research on focused attention has involved either the auditory or the visual modality. For reasons that are not altogether clear, most of the studies of focused attention carried out during the 1950s and 1960s were on auditory attention, whereas the emphasis in more recent years has shifted to visual attention.

Focused auditory attention

One of the characteristics of experimental psychologists is their ability to invent problems where none was previously thought to exist. When you are at a cocktail party (or any other kind of party), you almost certainly find that you are only able to attend to one conversation while ignoring all of the others going on at the same time. You usually listen to the conversation of the person or people nearest to you. However, if you hear your name mentioned in another conversation further away, then you will probably divert your attention in order to discover what is being said about you.

This ability to follow one particular conversation when there are several going on within earshot is one that we typically take for granted. To Colin Cherry, working at the Massachusetts Institute of Technology in the early 1950s, this ability constituted what he described as the "cocktail party problem". Cherry wanted to know what was involved in selective attention. In order to do that, he first of all had to develop some novel experimental techniques.

Cherry's experiments. In some of his early experiments, Cherry (1953) presented two different messages simultaneously on the same audio tape spoken by the same person. The subject's task was to follow just one message while ignoring the other. Since the messages were presented to both ears, this may be referred to as the *binaural task*. To Cherry's surprise, it was very difficult to perform this task successfully, and some of the subjects resorted to closing their eyes in order to assist concentration. Subjects usually managed to disentangle the two messages, but some sections of the tape had to be played up to 20 times before this happened. We can conclude that selective attention does not function very well when two messages can be separated only on the basis of meaning.

If people do not generally use meaning to tune in to one conversation rather than another, what do they use? The answer came when Cherry (1953) moved on to the *dichotic listening task*, in which headphones were used to present one message to the left ear and a different message to the right ear. The subjects were given the task of repeating back, or "shadowing", one of the messages while they were listening. Cherry discovered that subjects now experienced no problem in following one message while ignoring the other one, even when the two messages were spoken in the same voice. It thus appears that at least part of the solution to the cocktail party problem is that people are skilful at using the direction from which the target conversation is coming in order to facilitate the process of selective attention.

If people are very good at selecting or attending to one message while ignoring a second, then we would expect them to be able to report relatively little about the non-shadowed or unattended message. In fact, the subjects displayed an astonishing degree of ignorance concerning the non-shadowed message. When this message was in German, most of the subjects reported that they really had no idea what it was about but assumed it had been spoken in English. When the non-shadowed message consisted entirely of reversed speech, most people reported that it had been in normal speech, although a few claimed that there had been "something queer about it". Even when the non-shadowed message was in normal English speech, not a single word or phrase in it could be reported immediately after the end of the message.

In spite of all of these failures to report on any of the major characteristics of the non-shadowed message, some things about this message were detected. Simple physical characteristics such as the sex of the speaker and the intensity of sound were noticed, as was the unexpected insertion of a pure tone into the middle of the speech.

Cherry's pioneering research convinced him that selective attention (at least in the auditory modality) was a very efficient process. What was wanted could be selected with apparent ease from what was not wanted on the basis of its physical characteristics (i.e. its location, its intensity, and so on).

Broadbent's filter theory. Donald Broadbent (1958) believed that Cherry's findings were important, and so he proposed a theory of attention which attempted to account for them and for other findings (see the figure below).

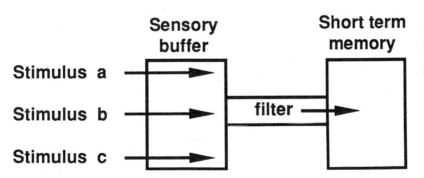

A diagrammatic representation of Broadbent's theory of attention

He argued that information from all of the stimuli presented at any given time enters a sensory buffer. One of the inputs is then selected on the basis of its physical characteristics for further processing by being allowed to pass through a filter. Because we have only a limited capacity to process information, this filter is designed to prevent the information-processing system from becoming overloaded. The inputs not initially selected by the filter remain briefly in the sensory buffer, and if they are not processed they decay rapidly.

This theory handles Cherry's main findings. The importance of the physical characteristics of stimuli is recognised in the mode of functioning of the filter mechanism. In the dichotic listening task, the filter simply selects one of the two messages on the basis of the most salient difference in their physical characteristics (i.e. ear of arrival). The content of the non-shadowed or unattended message cannot be reported because it is rejected by the filter and thus receives minimal processing.

Dichotic listening revisited. Broadbent (1958) assumed that the filter rejected the non-shadowed or unattended message at an early stage of processing, and the initial research seemed to support that assumption. However, the early studies all used people who were unfamiliar with shadowing and so found it very difficult and demanding. Furthermore, the notion that there is practically no processing of the unattended message was originally based upon subjects' reports after the entire message had been played. It is possible that the unattended message is analysed reasonably thoroughly, but that subjects typically forget what was in the message when questioned at a later time. Alternatively, much analysis of the unattended message might occur below the level of conscious awareness.

More recent research has indicated that these factors are important. The effects of practice were investigated by comparing the performance of inexperienced subjects with that of a highly experienced subject. A major researcher on dichotic listening, Neville Moray, with enormous experience of the shadowing task took part in the experiment. The task was to detect digits appearing on either the shadowed or the non-shadowed message. The naive subjects were able to detect only 8% of the digits appearing on the non-shadowed message, whereas Moray successfully detected 67% of the digits (Underwood, 1974). Thus, the amount of processing of the unattended message appears to depend greatly on the extent to which the shadowing task uses up available processing capacity. Moray was so familiar with shadowing that it was relatively undemanding for him.

Is it possible for the meaning of words on the unattended message to be processed without the listener being aware of it? While it may sound unlikely, the answer appears to be "Yes". Consider, for example, a study reported by von Wright, Anderson, and Stenman (1975). During the initial part of the experiment, their subjects learned that the Finnish word for 'suitable' was followed by an electric shock. Subsequently, the shocked word was presented in the unattended message, but this time it was not paired with shock. Although the subjects were not consciously aware that the previously shocked word had been presented, it nevertheless produced a noticeable galvanic skin response—sweating on the palm of the hand indicating an emotional reaction. This suggests that information on the unattended message can be processed for meaning below the level of conscious awareness.

Such findings provided the death-knell for Broadbent's original theory. It is now indisputable that the unattended message can be processed far more thoroughly than was allowed for in his theory. Accordingly, we must consider alternative theories which may provide more adequate accounts of the phenomena of selective attention.

Other theoretical positions.   Broadbent's argument proposed a bot-tle-neck in information processing, and he located this bottle-neck in the filter at an early stage of processing. Other theorists agreed with Broad-bent that there was indeed a bottle-neck, but they disagreed about its location. Anne Treisman (1964) proposed an attenuation theory, in which the unattended message was processed less thoroughly than the attended one, but was usually processed to a greater extent than was allowed for in Broadbent's theory. In other words, processing of the unattended message was attenuated or reduced to a greater or lesser extent depending on the demands on the limited capacity processing system. Treisman's theory can be regarded as assuming the existence of a "leaky" filter, with selective attention being less efficient than Broadbent had assumed.

Let us consider Treisman's theory in a little more detail. She suggested that messages are processed in a systematic way, beginning with analysis of physical characteristics, syllabic pattern, and individual words. After that, grammatical structure and meaning are processed. It will often happen that there is insufficient processing capacity to permit a full analysis of unattended stimuli. In that case, later analyses will be omitted. This theory neatly predicts that it will usually be the physical charac-teristics of unattended inputs which are remembered rather than their meaning.

A more radical departure from Broadbent's position was proposed by Anthony and Diana Deutsch (1963). They claimed that all inputs are fully analysed before any selection occurs. The bottle-neck or filter is thus placed late in the information-processing system, immediately before a response is made. Selection at that late stage is based on the relative importance of the inputs.

Deciding definitively between the theoretical positions of Treisman and of Deutsch and Deutsch has not really been possible. Treisman's theory seems more plausible in some ways. The assumption made by Deutsch and Deutsch that all stimuli are analysed completely, but that most of the analysed information is lost almost immediately, seems rather uneconom-ical. Physiological evidence supports Treisman. When a measure of

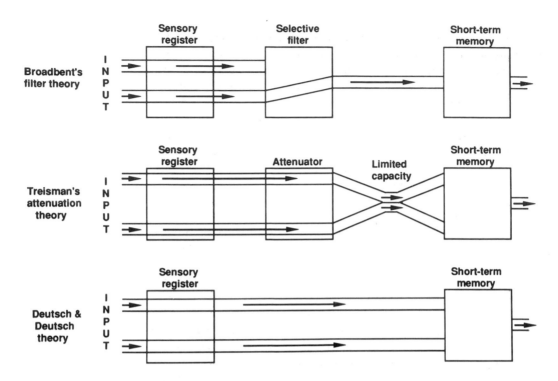

Broadbent's filter theory

INPUT

Sensory register — Selective filter — Short-term memory

Treisman's attenuation theory

INPUT

Sensory register — Attenuator — Limited capacity — Short-term memory

Deutsch & Deutsch theory

INPUT

Sensory register — Short-term memory

A diagrammatic representation contrasting Broadbent's theory (top); Treisman's theory (middle); and Deutsch & Deutsch's theory (bottom).

brain-wave activity known as the evoked potential is recorded, it typically shows that the initial response to the unattended message is much weaker than the response to the attended message, suggesting attenuated processing of the unattended message. On the other hand, other evidence supports Deutsch and Deutsch. In particular, studies such as the one by von Wright et al. (1975) seem to indicate that the meaning of words on the unattended message can sometimes be processed, exactly as predicted by Deutsch and Deutsch.

A reasonable compromise position was adopted by Johnston and Heinz (1978). They argued that the theories we have considered so far all suffer from the disadvantage that they are too *inflexible*. According to them, selection can occur at several different stages in processing. The precise stage at which selection takes place is usually as early in processing as possible in the light of the requirements of the current task. This is because the demands on processing capacity increase progressively, the more that selection is delayed.

These theoretical ideas were tested by Johnston and Heinz (1979). They presented target words which had to be shadowed or repeated back to both ears, and at the same time they presented non-target words to both ears. In one condition, the targets were spoken in a male voice and the non-targets in a female voice. In the other condition, targets and non-targets were spoken in the same male voice. It should be possible to select out the target words in the former condition simply on the basis of sensory information, whereas selection in the latter condition can occur only on the basis of the subsequent processing of meaning. According to the theory of Johnston and Heinz (1978), non-target words should be more thoroughly processed in the latter condition. Two of the findings confirmed this prediction: more processing resources were used in the latter than in the former condition, and subsequent recall of the non-target words was greater in the latter condition.

Focused visual attention

Focused visual attention is often likened to a spotlight. As with the light thrown by a spot, everything within a relatively small area can be seen very clearly, but anything that does not fall within the spotlight's beam is considerably more difficult to see. Most spotlights have adjustable beams, so that the area covered by the beam can be increased or decreased at will. Many theorists have argued that the same is true of visual attention.

LaBerge (1983) explored the notion that visual attention operates like an adjustable beam. In one experiment he presented five-letter words, and the subjects were asked either to focus on the middle letter of the word (categorise the middle letter) or on the entire word (categorise the word). He hoped that these two tasks would produce differences in the width of the attentional beam. In order to test this, subjects were asked to respond as rapidly as possible to a visual signal or probe which could appear in the spatial position of any of the five letters.

The findings from this study by LaBerge (1983) are shown in the diagram below. In order to make sense of them, it is necessary to assume that the probe was responded to faster when it fell within the central attentional beam than when it did not. The results suggest, therefore, that

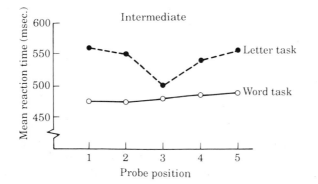

Mean reaction time to the probe stimulus, as a function of probe position. The probe was presented at the time that a letter string would have been presented.

the attentional spotlight can be either very narrow or rather broad depending on the precise task requirements.

What happens to unattended visual stimuli? As is the case with unattended auditory stimuli, it appears that there is rather limited processing of such stimuli. This was shown in a somewhat complex experiment reported by Johnston and Dark (1985). They were interested in whether the task of identifying a blurred test word would be facilitated by the immediately prior presentation for between 60 and 500 milliseconds of a prime word which could be either the same as the test word or a word related in meaning to it. When the prime word was presented to the attended visual area, then both kinds of primes facilitated identification of the test word. This simply means that useful information about the shapes of the letters and about meaning was extracted from the prime word when it was attended. In contrast, prime words presented to the unattended visual area generally had no beneficial effect at all on identification of the test word. This suggests that very little information was extracted from the unattended prime word. Johnston and Dark (1986) reviewed the literature on focused visual attention and came to the following conclusion: "Stimulus processing outside the attentional spotlight is restricted mainly to simple physical features" (p. 56).

Anne Treisman (1988) put forward a *feature integration theory* of attended and unattended visual stimuli. This theory involves a distinction between *objects* and the *features* of objects (e.g. colour, size, outlines). Some of the key aspects of her feature integration theory are as follows:

- The visual features of objects in the environment are processed rapidly in parallel (i.e. all at the same time) without attention being required; this is the first stage of processing.
- The features are then combined to form objects (e.g. a red chair, a purple flower) by means of a slow, serial (i.e. one after another) process; this is the second stage of processing.
- Focused attention on the location of an object can provide the "glue" which permits objects to be formed from combined features.
- Features can also be combined on the basis of stored knowledge (e.g. strawberries are red).
- In the absence of focused attention or relevant stored knowledge, features will be combined in a random fashion; this can produce odd combinations of features known as *illusory conjunctions*.

Feature integration theory can be tested by considering the length of time taken to detect a target stimulus in a display. If the target stimulus is defined in terms of a single feature (e.g. something blue), then only the first stage of processing should be required. Since the first stage of processing occurs in parallel, the speed of detection should scarcely be affected by the number of items in the display. The results should be quite different, however, if the target is an object defined by a combination of features (e.g. a green letter T). In this case, the second stage of processing and focused attention would be involved. Since focused attention operates in a serial fashion, detection speed should be much slower when there are several items in the visual display than when there are few. Both of these findings were reported by Treisman and Gelade (1980).

Feature integration theory also leads to the prediction that illusory conjunctions or incorrect combinations of features should occur when attention is not focused on the critical part of a display, but should not occur when stimuli are presented to focal attention. Precisely this pattern of results was reported in a later study by Treisman and Schmidt (1982).

In spite of the successes of feature integration theory, there are increasing signs that it is over-simplified (see Humphreys and Bruce, 1989). According to feature integration theory, features are usually combined as a result of focused attention. However, there are several studies in which that was not the case. It appears that feature combination via focused attention may be needed only when there are particular problems in discriminating between target and non-target stimuli. When the discrimination is an easy one, then the rapid, parallel, first stage of processing may be sufficient to allow the target to be detected.

Divided attention

So far we have considered what happens when we try to attend to one stimulus while ignoring a second one. Attention theorists are also interested in the very different situation where we attempt to do two things at once. In this situation attention must be allocated to both tasks—i.e. it must be divided between them.

Can we do two things at once? Common sense tells us that it all depends on what "things" we are referring to. A motorist who has been driving for many years can usually drive and hold a conversation at the same time, whereas it is notoriously difficult to rub your stomach with one hand while patting your head with the other. The first task for psychologists interested in focused attention was to investigate the factors responsible for allowing (or not allowing) two tasks to be carried out successfully. It is to these factors that we turn now, before considering the theoretical implications of the findings.

"APPARENTLY, SOME PEOPLE CAN'T DO TWO THINGS AT ONCE..."   "OH REALLY? THATS.....OOOF!!..."

Task difficulty

Perhaps the most obvious factor determining how well we can perform two tasks together is their level of difficulty. Most of us can walk and talk at the same time, because both activities are so easy, but very few of us could read a complicated textbook while doing difficult mental arithmetic (e.g. $46 \times 62 = ?$).

Psychologists agree that task difficulty is an important factor, but they would point out that the notion of "task difficulty" is a rather vague one. One task can clearly be more difficult than another in a number of ways, but it is not always clear which of two tasks is the more difficult one (e. g. is it harder to write a letter or listen to the radio?). More importantly, a task that is difficult for one person may be very straightforward for another. Driving a car seems almost impossibly difficult when you are first learning to drive, but it becomes very easy as a result of experience and practice.

In spite of these complications, there is strong evidence that task difficulty can have a major impact on the ability to do two tasks at the same time. For example, consider a study using the shadowing task described earlier in the chapter. Subjects were asked to detect specified target words in the non-shadowed message while shadowing a second message. More targets were detected by subjects when the shadowed message was simple than when it was complex (Sullivan, 1976).

When we consider task difficulty, we should not only consider the difficulty of each of the tasks separately. The requirement to perform two tasks together may produce fresh demands or difficulties because of the need for co-ordination and avoidance of interference. Duncan (1979) asked his subjects to respond as rapidly as possible to two successive stimuli, one of which involved a left-hand response while the other involved a right-hand response. The relationship between the location of each stimulus and the required response was either *corresponding*, in which case the right-most stimulus called for response by the right-most finger, and the left-most stimulus required response by the left-most finger. The opposite pattern was *crossed*, in which case the right-most stimulus was responded to by the left-most finger and the left-most stimulus by the right-most finger. Subjects performed very poorly when the relationship between one stimulus and its response was corresponding, whereas the relationship between the other stimulus and its response was crossed. As might be expected, there appeared to be considerable confusion under these conditions.

Practice

We all know the saying, "Practice makes perfect", and it seems very relevant to studies of divided attention. While experienced motorists can easily drive and converse at the same time, learner drivers are likely to finish up in the ditch if they start talking while struggling with the demands of driving! A formal demonstration of the value of practice was provided in striking fashion by Spelke, Hirst, and Neisser (1976). Their subjects were two students (Diane and John) who were given approximately 90 hours of training on a variety of tasks. The students were first of all asked to read short stories for comprehension while writing down words at dictation. To begin with, their reading speed and their handwriting during dictation both suffered substantially. After 30 hours of practice, however, their reading speed and comprehension had both improved up to the levels they displayed when not taking dictation, and in addition their handwriting was also of better quality.

There was a slightly curious aspect of Diane and John's otherwise very impressive level of performance. They had been given thousands of words for dictation, but they were able to recall only a tiny fraction of them. This suggested to Spelke et al. (1976) that their subjects might not be attending to the meanings of the words they were writing down at dictation. The clearest evidence for this was that neither Diane nor John noticed when 20 successive dictated words all belonged to the same category (e.g. articles of furniture). However, with extra training they were able to write down the names of the categories to which the dictated words belonged while maintaining their normal levels of reading speed and comprehension.

Task similarity

When we try to think of everyday activities that can be performed together reasonably easily, most of the examples that come to mind tend to involve dissimilar activities (e.g. walking and listening to a personal stereo). The notion that it is difficult to carry out two rather similar tasks at the same time would help to explain why it is so difficult to rub your stomach with one hand while patting your head with the other. It may well be that the inability to report much about the non-shadowed message in the shadowing situation described earlier in the chapter is due to the great similarity between the two stimulus inputs: very often, they are both coherent English prose passages, and they are both presented in the auditory modality.

Some of these ideas were explored by Allport, Antonis, and Reynolds (1972). They gave their subjects the task of shadowing auditorily presented prose passages while learning auditorily presented words. The subjects displayed no subsequent ability at all to recognise the words in a memory test. Very different results were obtained, however, when the two tasks were made dissimilar by combining the standard shadowing task with the task of learning pictorial information. This time recognition memory was extremely good, with approximately 90% of the pictures being recognised.

It is important to note that two tasks can be similar or dissimilar in a number of different ways. In particular, there is similarity of the stimuli in the two tasks, similarity of the internal processing operations, and similarity of responses. All three kinds of similarity have been found to affect combined performance of the two tasks, but the most striking evidence so far has come from studies in which stimulus similarity has been investigated. Allport et al. (1972) discovered that it was difficult to cope with two simultaneous auditory inputs, and Paul Kolers (1972) found that the same was true for two visual inputs. He invented a special headgear with a half-silvered mirror; it was designed so that the visual world in front of him and the visual world behind him were both available. Kolers found that it was easy to attend to whichever visual world he preferred, but it was impossible to attend to both visual worlds at the same time.

The importance of response similarity was shown by McLeod (1977). One of his tasks was continuous tracking, which involved following a moving visual target with one hand, and the other task involved identifying tones. Some of the subjects responded vocally to the tones, whereas others used the hand not involved in the tracking task. Performance on the tracking task was worse when there was high response similarity (manual responses on both tasks) than when there was low response similarity (manual responses on the tracking task but vocal responses on the tone-identification task).

Theoretical considerations

We have seen that the extent to which two tasks can be performed successfully together depends on a variety of factors. As a rule of thumb, two dissimilar, highly practised, and simple tasks can typically be performed well together, whereas two similar, novel, and complex tasks cannot. In addition, having to perform two tasks together rather than separately frequently produces entirely new problems of co-ordination. For example, moving your forefinger in front of you in a circular fashion is very easy. It is also easy to move both forefingers around in a circular fashion if they both move in the same direction (i.e. both clockwise or anti-clockwise). It is more difficult, however, to move one forefinger clockwise around an imaginary circle while the other forefinger moves anti-clockwise, because the two tasks interfere with each other and resist co-ordination. The study by Duncan (1979) discussed above illustrates the same point.

There is fairly general agreement on the major factors influencing performance on divided attention tasks, but there has been much disagreement about the proper theoretical explanation. The simplest view is the *central capacity interference theory*, which has been favoured by Norman and Bobrow (1975) and by several other theorists. The crucial assumptions of this theory are that there is some central capacity (attention or effort) which possesses rather limited resources, and that the ability to perform two tasks together depends upon the demands placed on those resources by the two tasks. Quite simply, performance will be poor if the two tasks require more resources than are available, whereas the tasks can be performed successfully together if their combined demands for resources are less than the total resources of the central capacity.

How does the central capacity interference theory account for the main findings from studies of divided attention? The fact that task difficulty is an important factor poses no problem for the theory, because task difficulty is defined simply as the demands placed by the task on the resources of the central capacity. The finding that two reasonably demanding tasks can sometimes be performed successfully together (e.g. reading for comprehension and writing at dictation; Spelke et al., 1976) seems contrary to the spirit of the central capacity theory. This is because complex tasks impose heavy demands on central resources, and this should lead to disruption of performance. The counter-argument is that complex tasks can usually only be performed well together after a substantial amount of practice. Tasks are usually tackled in a more efficient way after practice, and thus the demands on central resources are reduced. An extreme version of this argument was proposed by Shiffrin and Schneider (1977).

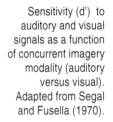

Sensitivity (d') to auditory and visual signals as a function of concurrent imagery modality (auditory versus visual). Adapted from Segal and Fusella (1970).

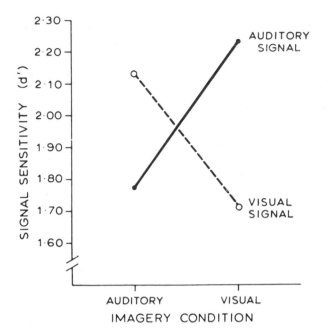

They claimed that prolonged practice can lead to the development of automatic processes which allegedly make no demands on central capacity.

While the central capacity interference theory can account for the effects of task difficulty and practice, it is considerably embarrassed by some of the effects of task similarity. This can be seen if we consider a study by Segal and Fusella (1970). Their subjects had to detect a weak visual or auditory signal while maintaining a visual or an auditory image. Since there were two signal-detection tasks and two imagery tasks, there were four possible combinations of tasks, all of which were used by Segal and Fusella (1970).

The findings on the signal-detection task are shown in the figure above. Performance on the auditory signal task was better when it was combined with the visual imagery task than when it was combined with the auditory imagery task. According to central capacity theorists, this means that the visual imagery task is easier and less demanding of resources than the auditory imagery task. Inspection of the findings, however, for the visual signal task points to the opposite conclusion. Here performance was better when the visual signal task was combined with the auditory imagery task, suggesting that the auditory imagery task requires fewer resources than the visual imagery task. Thus, this simple demonstration of the importance of task similarity (in terms of whether both tasks use the same sense modality) cannot readily be explained by central capacity interference theorists. It should be noted that there are numerous other studies in which a similar pattern of results was obtained.

A very different theoretical position was taken by Alan Allport (1980) and others. They suggested that there are a number of different specific processing mechanisms, each of which has limited capacity. The advantage of this approach is that it allows us to make sense of the fact that the degree of similarity between two tasks plays a major role in determining how well they can be performed together. In essence, similar tasks compete for the same specific processing mechanisms, and this competition produces disruption of performance. On the other hand, dissimilar tasks make use of different mechanisms, and so will often not interfere with each other in any way.

We can perhaps clarify this theoretical approach, taking as an example driving a car and holding a conversation at the same time. Car driving requires a number of specific skills involving visual perception and motor responses, whereas holding a conversation involves language skills and the appropriate use of information stored in long-term memory. Theoretically, it is because such different skills are involved that the two activities can be combined so successfully. It would be unwise to argue that one of the theories discussed here is correct and the other is incorrect. Both theories provide good accounts of some of the evidence, and are probably both partially correct. According to Eysenck (1984), a theory combining some aspects of central capacity interference theory and of the specific mechanisms theory may prove to be more adequate than either theory on its own. There is a hierarchical structure of processes, with attention or the central processor at the top of the hierarchy and more specific processing resources below it. The effects of task difficulty are due largely to attention or the central processor, whereas the effects of similarity are due to the specific processing resources. Finally, the effects of practice occur because tasks that initially require extensive use of attention no longer do so after prolonged practice.

Automatic processing

We have seen in this chapter (especially in the work of Spelke et al., 1976) that practice can have a dramatic effect on performance. An increasingly popular way of accounting for some of the effects of practice is to argue that many processes become automatic if they are used very frequently. There has been some disagreement about the best definition of automaticity, but the following criteria have often been suggested:

- Automatic processes are fast.
- Automatic processes do not require attention.
- Automatic processes are unavoidable—that is, they always occur when an appropriate stimulus is presented.
- There is no conscious awareness of automatic processes.

This theoretical perspective provides a somewhat different interpretation of the experienced motorist's ability to drive and converse at the same time. Many of the components of driving (e.g. changing gear) may have become more or less automatic as a result of extensive practice, and the same is true of several aspects of the over-learned skills involved in the comprehension and production of speech. The development of automatic processes "saves" the very limited capacity of attention for other pressing tasks.

Some of the best known research on automatic processes was carried out by Schneider and Shiffrin (1977) and Shiffrin and Schneider (1977). Their basic experimental situation was one in which subjects memorised one, two, three, or four items (consonants or numbers); this was called the memory set. They were then shown a visual display containing one, two, three, or four items (consonants or numbers). Finally, they had to decide quickly whether there was any item that was common to the memory set and to the visual display. Of crucial importance was the distinction between *consistent* versus *varied mapping*. With consistent mapping, only consonants were used as members of the memory set, and only numbers were used as distractors in the visual display (or vice versa). According to Shiffrin and Schneider (1977), the subjects' years of practice at distinguishing between letters and numbers allowed them to perform the consistent-mapping task in an automatic fashion. With varied mapping, on the other hand, the memory set consisted of a mixture of consonants and numbers, and so did the visual display. In these circumstances, it should not be possible to use automatic processes.

The findings are set out in the figure on page 59. They show that there was a substantial difference in performance between performance under the consistent and varied mapping conditions. The number of items in the memory set and the visual display had very little effect on decision time with consistent mapping, but a rather large effect with varied mapping. According to Shiffrin and Schneider (1977), performance in the consistent-mapping condition reflects the use of fast automatic processes operating in parallel. On the other hand, performance in the varied mapping condition reflects the use of attentionally demanding controlled processes which operate in a serial fashion. The more items that need to be considered, the slower is the decision time.

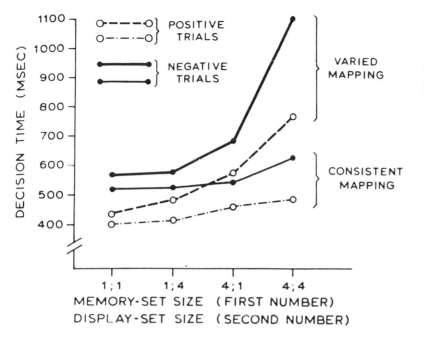

Response latency on a decision task as a function of memory-set size and consistent versus varied mapping.

Presumably automatic processes develop as the result of prolonged practice. This notion was investigated by Shiffrin and Schneider (1977). They used consistent mapping with the memory set items always being drawn from the consonants B to L and the distractors in the visual display always being drawn from the consonants Q to Z, or vice versa. The subjects received 2,100 trials, and the dramatic improvement in performance over those trials appeared to reflect the development of automatic processes. After these automatic processes had developed, there were a further 2,400 trials with the reverse consistent mapping. Thus, for example, if the memory set items had been drawn from the first half of the alphabet during the initial 2,100 trials, they were taken from the second half of the alphabet during the subsequent 2,400 trials. Reversing the consistent mapping greatly impaired performance. Indeed, the impairment was so great that it took almost 1,000 trials for performance to recover to its level at the very beginning of the experiment. This suggests that it is difficult to abandon automatic responses that have outlived their usefulness.

What are the relative advantages and disadvantages of automatic and attentional processes? The most obvious advantages of automatic over attentional processes are that they usually operate much more rapidly and that numerous automatic processes can take place at the same time. However, as we have just seen, automatic processes are at a disadvantage when there is any significant change in the environment or in the prevailing conditions, because they lack the adaptability and flexibility of attentional processes. All in all, the fact that we possess both automatic and attentional processes allows us to respond quickly and appropriately to most situations.

How exactly does automaticity develop through prolonged practice? According to Logan (1988), practice at responding to the same stimulus leads to the storage of a considerable amount of information about the stimulus, and about what to do with it. It is this stored knowledge which underlies automaticity: "Automaticity is memory retrieval: performance is automatic when it is based on a single-step direct-access retrieval of past solutions from memory" (p. 493). After prolonged practice at responding to a given stimulus, the appropriate response is stored in memory and can be accessed very rapidly.

One of the advantages of Logan's (1988) approach is that it helps us to make sense of the various criteria for automaticity. Automatic processes are fast because all that is needed is the retrieval of "past solutions" from long-term memory. Automatic processes do not require attentional resources because the retrieval of well-learned knowledge from memory is relatively effortless. Automatic processes are unavailable to conscious awareness because there are practically no processes intervening between the presentation of a stimulus and the retrieval of the appropriate response.

Are there any major problems with the theoretical distinction between automatic and attentional processes? The most important one is that many so-called "automatic" processes fail to satisfy all of the criteria for automaticity discussed above. The so-called "Stroop effect" provides an example of this (see next panel).

Absent-mindedness

The common everyday phenomenon of absent-mindedness or action slips—i.e. the performance of unintended actions—illustrates some of the processes discussed in this chapter. This is because, in general terms, attentional failures are involved in most action slips or cases of absent-mindedness.

Action slips have proved rather difficult to observe under laboratory conditions. Accordingly, the standard procedure has been to collect examples of action slips from everyday life and then to assign them to different categories. For example, James Reason (1979) asked several people to keep diaries recording any cases in which they behaved in an inappropriate way because of absent-mindedness. For example, one person admitted to the following: "I meant to get my car out, but as I passed through the back porch on my way to the garage I stopped to put on my wellington boots and gardening jacket as if to work in the garden" (Reason, 1979, p. 73).

The Stroop effect

Individual words are presented printed in different colours. Subjects have to name the colours. Where the words themselves are colour names (e.g. the word BLUE is printed in red), the naming of the colours is slowed down. As the Stroop effect occurs in spite of subjects' attempts to avoid attending to the colour word, it has been assumed that processing of the colour word happens automatically. It has been found, however, that the Stroop effect is much greater when the distracting colour word is in the same location as the to-be-named colour rather than in an adjacent location within the central fixation area (Kahneman & Henik, 1979). Automatic processes are supposed to be unavoidable, but this finding suggests that the Stroop effect does not always adhere to that criterion of automaticity.

What we have here are two over-learned and largely automatic action sequences (i.e. walking through the back porch, putting on gardening clothes) with a crucial decision point between them. The individual concerned could quite reasonably have walked through the porch on "automatic pilot", but should then have attended to what he was doing in order to make the correct decision as to whether to get the car out or prepare for gardening. Having made the decision, he could then have returned to relatively automatic processing.

According to Reason (1979), the above action slip represents a *test failure*, in which the progress of a planned sequence of actions is not monitored sufficiently at a crucial point in the sequence. Test failures accounted for approximately 20% of the action slips recorded by the diarists. The most numerous category of action slips (approximately 40% of the total) was that of *storage failures*, in which intentions and actions are forgotten or recalled incorrectly. Here is an example of a storage failure: "I started to pour a second kettle of boiling water into a teapot full of freshly made tea. I had no recollection of having just made it" (p. 74).

The other three categories of action slips discussed by Reason (1979) can be mentioned briefly:

- *Sub-routine failures* (18% of the errors) involve insertions, omissions, or re-orderings of the stages in an action sequence, as the following illustrates: "I sat down to do some work and before starting to write I put my hand up to my face to take my glasses off, but my fingers snapped together rather abruptly because I hadn't been wearing them in the first place" (p. 73).

- *Discrimination failures* (11% of the total) involve failures to discriminate between somewhat similar objects (e.g. shaving cream and toothpaste).
- *Program assembly failures* (5% of the errors) involve inappropriate combinations of actions (e.g. "I unwrapped a sweet, put the paper in my mouth, and threw the sweet into the waste bucket.")

How useful are diary studies? On the positive side, they do provide an indication of the major kinds of action slip which occur in everyday life. It is important to be able to identify the main categories of action slip for theoretical purposes. On the negative side, the percentage figures for the different kinds of action slips should not be taken too seriously for two reasons. First, there may be many action slips that are never detected, and are not recorded in the subjects' diaries. Secondly, it is extremely difficult to interpret the error percentages unless one knows the frequency of occasions on which a particular kind of action slip might have occurred but did not. For example, there may be relatively few discrimination failures simply because there are relatively few occasions in everyday life in which similar objects need to be discriminated from each other.

In spite of these problems with diary studies, some features of action slips emerge clearly. It is worth noting that the great majority of action slips occur during the performance of highly practised activities. This seems paradoxical in some ways, because practice typically leads to improvement in performance and to a reduction in the number of errors. According to Reason (1979), this paradox can be accounted for by distinguishing between a *closed-loop* or *feedback mode of control* involving attentional mechanisms, and an *open-loop mode of control*, in which performance is controlled by motor programs or other automatic processes. The closed-loop or feedback mode of control is used during the early stages of practice, but is increasingly replaced by the open-loop mode of control as practice continues.

The implication of Reason's (1979) theoretical position is that most cases of absent-mindedness occur because we rely on automatic processes (the open-loop mode of control) when we should be actively attending to the task in hand (i.e. using the closed-loop or feedback mode of control). The obvious implication is that we could eliminate absent-mindedness by paying full attention to everything we do. However, this would be a wasteful use of resources. What is actually the best strategy is to shift rapidly between automatic and attentional processes as circumstances require. That most of us do, in fact, adopt the best strategy is suggested by Reason's finding that his subjects (i.e. the diarists) produced an average of only one instance of absent- mindedness per day.

Many action slips (e.g. storage failures) occur because of a lack of memory of what has been done previously. This is precisely what we would expect if attentional failures are involved. As we saw earlier in the chapter, studies of focused auditory and visual attention have shown that relatively little information about unattended stimuli is stored away in long-term memory. Poor storage of information leads inevitably to poor ability to recall the information subsequently. Other action slips (e.g. test failures; programme assembly failures) occur because action is determined by a strong (but inappropriate) motor program rather than by a weaker (but appropriate) motor program. It is a characteristic of the open-loop mode of control that strong motor programs will be selected, so that the failure to select the weaker but appropriate motor program is due to a lack of attentional or closed-loop control at the decision point.

Vigilance

As was pointed out in the introduction, one interesting way of considering attention is in terms of people's ability to pay continuous attention to tasks which are monotonous, long-lasting, and involve the detection of occasional signals. Tasks possessing these characteristics are called "vigilance tasks". There are various jobs (e.g. maintaining radar watch on a submarine, inspecting goods coming off a production line) that resemble vigilance tasks, and it is important to understand some of the processes involved.

Systematic research in this area was initiated by Mackworth (1950). He made use of a clock pointer that moved on in a series of steps. The subjects were told to watch the pointer, and to report the relatively infrequent occasions on which it gave a double jump. In view of the tedious nature of this task, it is not surprising that Mackworth obtained clear evidence for a *vigilance decrement*—i.e. the probability of detecting the double jump or signal tended to decrease over time. Numerous other investigators have also found a vigilance decrement, and it represents the most obvious characteristic of performance on vigilance tasks.

It is perhaps natural to assume that the vigilance decrement occurs because the observer is gradually less able to maintain attention and so becomes less sensitive to the signals. However, as Broadbent (1971) pointed out, what is involved in the vigilance decrement is actually more complicated than that. The number of *false alarms* (i.e. the reported detections of signals when none is presented) tends to decrease during the course of a vigilance task, which indicates that observers become more cautious about reporting the presence of signals. It is possible to use information about detection rates and false alarms to provide independent measures of observer sensitivity and of his or her cautiousness in responding. When this is done, it is usually found that the vigilance decrement is due more to an increased reluctance to respond when a signal is presented than to a reduction in the observer's level of sensitivity to stimulation.

Reducing the decrement

From the practical point of view, it is obviously of major importance to discover ways in which the vigilance decrement can be avoided. In Mackworth's (1950) original research, he discovered that providing feedback or knowledge of results when a signal was either missed or correctly detected prevented the vigilance decrement from occurring. There are at least two possible reasons why knowledge of results was beneficial: first, it provided accurate information about the subject's performance and second it increased the level of motivation. Subsequent research has suggested that the effects of knowledge of results on vigilance performance are due to increased motivation rather than to the provision of information. For example, Nachreiner (1977) motivated some of his subjects by telling them that good performance on a vigilance task might lead to the offer of a well-paid part-time job. These highly motivated subjects did not exhibit vigilance decrement. Warm, Epps, and Ferguson (1974) found that simulated or "false" knowledge of results was as effective as genuine feedback in improving vigilance performance, suggesting that accurate information is not needed to improve performance.

In general terms, people who are wide awake are more physiologically aroused than those who are sleepy. They are also better at performing most tasks, including vigilance tasks. Since physiological arousal tends to fall during the course of most vigilance tasks, it seems likely that the level of physiological arousal may be an important factor in producing the vigilance decrement. There have also been several studies in which some of the subjects were exposed to high intensity white noise (i.e. a noise consisting of all sound frequencies and resembling hissing). Intense white noise increases physiological arousal, and it also typically reduces the vigilance decrement. Mullin and Corcoran (1977) investigated the effects of white noise on vigilance performance at eight in the morning and eight in the evening. Noise had a very beneficial effect on performance in the morning but not in the evening. Probably the morning subjects were sleepy and so benefited from the stimulating properties of the white noise, whereas the evening subjects were wide awake even in the absence of white noise.

One of the difficulties with vigilance research is that those subjects who perform well on one vigilance task often do not perform well on a different one—i.e. vigilance tasks generally correlate poorly with each other. We cannot, therefore, be generally confident that findings obtained with a particular vigilance task can be replicated in other vigilance tasks. As yet, there is little agreement as to the crucial ways in which vigilance tasks differ from each other. However, as Eysenck (1988) pointed out:

> There are various obvious differences among vigilance tasks. These include the modality of stimulus presentation (usually visual or auditory), the rate at which signals are presented, the predictability of when stimuli will be presented, and the difficulty of the discrimination between the signal-present and the signal-absent environments. It is, indeed, the case that correlations between vigilance tasks resembling each other in terms of these characteristics are usually much higher than those between vigilance tasks selected at random. [pp. 111-112].

In recent years there has been a decline in research on vigilance and there are probably two main reasons for this. First, it has proved rather difficult to discover much about attentional processes and mechanisms by studying vigilance performance. Secondly, there are increasingly few jobs that correspond closely to the demands of traditional vigilance tasks, in which an essentially passive observer awaits the presentation of a signal. With advances in computer and other technology, it is more and more the case that workers have an active involvement in most tasks, and can interrogate the systems with which they are working. There are now fewer practical implications of vigilance research than used to be the case.

Summary: Attention

- Attention research distinguishes between studies of focused or selective attention—processing and responding to only one input—and studies of divided attention—processing all the inputs as well as possible. In both cases, two or more sets of stimuli are presented simultaneously.
- Many studies of focused attention in the auditory modality have suggested that people are very good at attending to one auditory input while ignoring all irrelevant auditory inputs. However sensitive measures have revealed that some processing of the meaning of the unattended message may take place.

- There has been much theoretical controversy about the proper interpretation of the findings on selective attention in studies of focused auditory attention. The most reasonable position argues that people generally process as much of the "unattended" input as they need to identify correctly which input is to be attended to.
- The investigation of focused visual attention has led to similar findings. It appears that visual attention can be compared to a spotlight with a variable beam. Visual stimuli outside the attentional beam receive only minimal processing, especially of their meaning.
- Research on divided attention indicates that we can sometimes perform two tasks together with no apparent problem, whereas other pairs of tasks are virtually impossible to perform at the same time.
- There are two main theoretical viewpoints in the area of divided attention research. One is central capacity interference theory. The other proposes that there are actually several different specific processing mechanisms, all possessing limited capacity. A compromise position seems likely, with both a general attentional system and more specific processing mechanisms. This theory would be able to account reasonably well for the effects of task difficulty, task similarity, and practice on performance in studies of divided attention.
- Why does practice have such beneficial effects on performance? Practice appears to lead to the development of automatic processes, that are free from the capacity limitations that characterise attention.
- An over-reliance on automatic processes can lead to absent-mindedness.
- Vigilance tasks require attention. There is usually a progressive deterioration of performance over time, known as the vigilance decrement, but it is not yet clear which attentional mechanisms produce this.

Further reading

The topic of attention is dealt with at length in M. W. Eysenck and M. Keane (1990), *Cognitive Psychology: A Student's Handbook* (Hove, U.K.: Lawrence Erlbaum Associates Ltd.). A scholarly review of attention research and theory is to be found in W. A. Johnston and V. J. Dark (1986), Selective attention, *Annual Review of Psychology, 37,* 43–75. The interesting phenomenon of absent-mindedness is discussed by J. T. Reason and K. Mycielska (1982), *The Psychology of Mental Lapses and Everyday Errors* (Englewood Cliffs, N. J.: Prentice-Hall). Vigilance is discussed by M. W. Eysenck (1982a), *Attention and Arousal: Cognition and Performance* (Berlin: Springer).

Memory 4

H ow important is memory to normal human functioning? Imagine if we were without it. We would not recognise anyone or anything as familiar. We would not be able to talk, read, or write, because we would remember nothing about language. Experience would have taught us nothing, and we would have the same lack of knowledge that characterises new-born infants.

We use memory for an impressive variety of purposes. It enables us to keep track of conversations, to remember telephone numbers for the length of time it takes to dial them, to write essays in examinations, to make sense of what we read, and to recognise the faces of people we know. The very richness of memory functioning has suggested to many psychologists that we must possess not a single memory system but rather a number of different memory systems. This chapter aims to explore in detail some of the proposed sub-divisions of human memory.

Memory theorists usually assume that there is a major distinction between *storage* and *retrieval*. At the time of learning, some of the presented information is stored away within the memory system, and subsequently this information may or may not be retrieved or remembered. In other words, memory theorists need to concern themselves with the processes occurring at the time of input or storage, and they also need to investigate what happens at the time of output or retrieval. During the course of this chapter, we will be considering the events occurring at both storage and retrieval.

The ultimate goal of memory research is to produce theoretical accounts of memory which are of practical use. For example, it would be of great value if the memory problems suffered by amnesics and others could be reduced by means of the application of sound psychological principles. We have not reached that point as yet, but the present state of play in applying memory research to practical problems is dealt with towards the end of the chapter.

Short-term and long-term memory

William James, brother of the novelist Henry James, was one of the greatest psychologists of the nineteenth century. He argued that we should distinguish between two kinds of memory which he referred to as *primary memory* and *secondary memory*. Primary memory is basically the psychological present, and consists of what is currently happening or what has just happened. Secondary memory relates to the psychological past. It deals with our recollection of events which may have happened days, weeks, or even years ago.

In more recent times, many theorists have distinguished between a short-term memory store (James's primary memory) and a long-term memory store (James's secondary memory). Short-term memory is rather fragile and short-lived, and is used when we try to remember a telephone number for a few seconds or when we follow someone else's conversation. Long-term memory is more durable, and is used when we remember our own telephone number or when we look back over the events of the day.

Evidence to support this distinction between short-term and long-term memory stores has been obtained from brain-damaged patients (see Chapter 1). If we discover that some of these patients have poor short-term memory but good long-term memory, whereas others have good short-term memory but poor long-term memory, then this would indicate that there are at least two separate memory stores. Both sorts of patients have been identified. KF was a patient who had suffered brain damage following a motor-cycle accident. His long-term learning and memory were reasonably good, but his short-term memory was grossly impaired (Shal-

William James (1842–1910). An American psychologist and philosopher who also received medical training. He spent much of his career at Harvard University, where he was first of all a professor of philosophy, then a professor of psychology, and finally a professor of philosophy again. His major impact on psychology came through his book, *Principles of Psychology*, which was published in 1890. It can be reasonably claimed that this was the first book to consider psychology from the cognitive perspective; as such, it was the forerunner of developments in psychology which occurred several decades later. James's training provided him with an unusually broad approach to psychology, but perhaps prevented him from establishing a coherent theoretical position.

lice and Warrington, 1970). In contrast, patients who have become amnesic as a result of chronic alcoholism (a condition known as Korsakoff's syndrome) have good short-term memory (e.g. they can hold reasonably normal conversations), but they have major problems with long-term memory (e.g. they might re-read a newspaper without realising that they have just read it).

The multi-store approach

Richard Atkinson and Richard Shiffrin (1968) used the distinction between the short-term and long-term memory stores as the basis for developing the *multi-store model of memory* (diagram at the bottom of the page). They argued that input information is initially received by sensory registers or modality-specific stores. Visual stimuli go to a special visual store (the *iconic store*), auditory stimuli go to a special auditory store (the *echoic store*), and so on for each of the sense modalities. Information in these modality-specific stores lasts for short periods of time—up to a second or two. Here is an everyday example of the echoic store in operation: you are reading a newspaper. Someone asks you a question. You start to say, "Pardon?", but then realise that you know what they have said by replaying it to yourself in the echoic store. Some of the information in the modality-specific stores is attended to and so receives further processing in the short-term store. Any information in the modality-specific stores which is not selected in this way simply decays rapidly.

The short-term store has a very limited capacity of not more than about six or seven items, and the information in the store is in a fragile state. These two characteristics of limited capacity and fragility are clearly apparent if you think of remembering a phone number while you dial it. It is very difficult to remember long phone numbers, and the slightest distraction can cause you to forget the number completely.

Rehearsal is the main process occurring in the short-term store. Rehearsed information is transferred to the long-term store during the time that it is being rehearsed. Unrehearsed items are forgotten as a result of displacement. This can be understood if you think of the short-term store as a small box that can hold only a small number of items. When the box

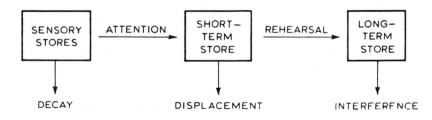

The multi-store model of memory.

or store is full, new items can only be put in by displacing or removing one or more of the items currently in the box or store.

The word "item" in this context needs defining. According to George Miller (1956), only approximately seven items or *chunks* can be stored in short-term memory, with each chunk consisting of a familiar unit of information based on previous learning. It follows that the capacity of short-term memory should be only approximately seven words if some-one tries to remember a list of unrelated words in the correct order (this is known as the word span). However, the capacity should be seven phrases (and far in excess of seven words) if the same person tries to remember a list of phrases. Evidence indicating that the capacity of short-term memory is less variable when measured in chunks rather than words was obtained by Herbert Simon (1974), the Nobel-prize-winning economist and psychologist. He found that the memory span was 7 words for unrelated words, whereas it was 22 words for 8-word phrases. These figures correspond to seven and three chunks, respectively.

The long-term store differs markedly from the short-term store in that it has essentially unlimited capacity. The reasons for forgetting from the short-term store are dealt with fully later in the chapter, but Atkinson and Shiffrin claimed that forgetting often occurs because of confusion among similar long-term memories. While they realised that forgetting could occur for other reasons, they argued that nearly all forgetting from long-term memory is due to an inability to find the appropriate memory trace rather than to the disappearance of the trace from the memory system.

The key contribution made by Atkinson and Shiffrin was the notion that there are three quite separate kinds of memory store: modality-specific stores, the short-term store, and the long-term store. These stores differ in terms of how long information is stored in them, in their storage capacity, and in terms of the way in which information is forgotten. Some of the limitations of the multi-store approach are discussed in the following sections.

Short-term storage: working memory

According to Atkinson and Shiffrin (1968), the long-term storage of information usually depends on the amount of rehearsal: the greater the amount of rehearsal of to-be-learned information, the better that long-term memory becomes. They also pointed out that the transfer of information from the short-term store to the long-term store could occur as a result of coding, by which they meant adding extra information from the long-term store to the presented information. While Atkinson and Shiffrin thus claimed that long-term memories can be formed through either rehearsal or coding, their emphasis was on rehearsal. This emphasis seems somewhat misplaced if we consider how we normally learn things every day. It is true that we sometimes say things over to ourselves as an aid to memory, but most people probably devote only a very small fraction of their time to rehearsal.

A more realistic theoretical position was put forward by Alan Baddeley and Graham Hitch (1974). They proposed that the concept of the short-term store should be replaced by that of *working memory*. Working memory consists of the following major components:

- A modality-free central executive, which is virtually synonymous with attention.
- An articulatory loop, which can be regarded as a verbal rehearsal system; it resembles an inner voice.
- A visuo-spatial sketch pad, which is a visual and/or spatial rehearsal system; it resembles an inner eye.

There are two rehearsal systems (the articulatory loop and the visuo-spatial sketch pad) which can be used depending on the kind of information that needs to be rehearsed. The central executive is an attentional system which plays a part in determining whether or not the rehearsal systems are used.

For present purposes, it is important to focus on the significant differences between the working memory model and the multi-store approach to short-term memory. The most obvious difference is that verbal rehearsal is reduced in importance: it takes place in only one out of the three components of working memory (i.e. the articulatory loop), whereas in the multi-store model it was the major function of the short-term store.

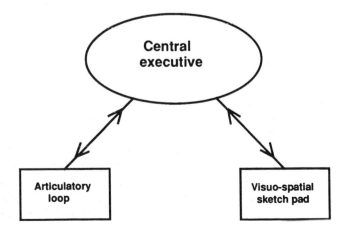

The lesser role accorded to verbal rehearsal in the working memory model makes it clear that there are several different forms of processing (related to the various components of working memory) which can be used when to-be-learned information is presented.

Research on the working memory model is still proceeding, but the characteristics of the articulatory loop are already reasonably clear. The loop is used if you are trying to remember a telephone number for a few seconds. The articulatory loop or inner voice has strictly limited capacity. Its capacity is equivalent to the amount of verbal information that can be articulated in approximately two seconds. As a consequence, it is harder for someone who has a fluent knowledge of both English and Welsh to remember Welsh telephone numbers than English ones, because Welsh numbers take longer to rehearse or say aloud.

Long-term memory: episodic versus semantic

Long-term memory contains a huge amount of very diverse information. We know what we did yesterday, what happened on our last summer holiday, that 2 + 2 = 4, that Leonardo da Vinci was a painter, and that Cointreau is a kind of liqueur.

Atkinson and Shiffrin (1968) claimed that all of this knowledge was contained in the same long-term store, but this seems unlikely. An alternative suggestion was put forward in 1972 by Endel Tulving, a psychologist born in Estonia but now working in North America. He argued that there is a major distinction which should be drawn between *episodic memory* and *semantic memory*. Episodic memory can best be thought of as memory for autobiographical or personal events that have happened to you. Remembering a particular examination that you have taken or a romantic encounter are two examples of episodic memory.

Semantic memory consists of the organised knowledge that we possess about language and about the world. Knowing that chairs are for sitting on and that it is colder in the winter than in the summer are two items of information that are stored in semantic memory. In general terms, semantic memories lack the specific information about time and place that typically characterises episodic memories. If you remember something that happened to you in London last Tuesday, then your memory is episodic rather than semantic.

Most laboratory studies of human memory have investigated episodic rather than semantic memory. For example, a list of words is presented to a subject in the laboratory. A recognition-memory test follows and includes the word "chair". The subject is in effect being asked whether the word "chair" was presented to him or her in the laboratory a little earlier.

Semantic memory lacking this autobiographical flavour would be tested by asking the subject whether he or she recognised that "chair" is a word in the English language.

The distinction between episodic and semantic memory makes intuitive sense. However, there is a strong suspicion that the two kinds of memory are not entirely separate from each other, and even Endel Tulving admits that the two memory systems are highly inter-dependent. For example, our semantic knowledge of chairs has developed as a result of our specific experiences with chairs, and the way in which information about a particular chair is processed depends in part upon our knowledge of chairs stored in semantic memory. Nevertheless, episodic and semantic memory can usefully be distinguished, provided that it is remembered that they are closely inter-connected.

Some theorists (e.g. Parkin, 1982) have argued that amnesic patients provide the strongest evidence for the distinction between episodic and semantic memory. Amnesic patients have largely unimpaired language skills, including vocabulary and grammar, and they perform at approximately the normal level in most intelligence tests. These skills suggest that their semantic memory is essentially intact. In contrast, they frequently forget what has happened to them hours or days earlier, which suggests a severe deficit in the ability to store new information in episodic memory. However, there is a flaw in this argument. Language and the abilities required to perform well in intelligence tests are nearly always acquired *before* the onset of amnesia, whereas conventional tests of episodic memory are based on information acquired *after* the onset of amnesia. In fact, the evidence suggests that amnesic patients have a reasonably good recollection of semantic and episodic memories established before the onset of amnesia, but rather poor memory for semantic and episodic information encountered afterwards. An implication is that episodic and semantic memory are not as different as Parkin (1982) and others have assumed.

Long-term memory: declarative and procedural knowledge

In spite of the differences between them, both episodic and semantic memory involve what has been called *declarative knowledge*. Perhaps the simplest way of defining declarative knowledge is to say that it is concerned with *knowing that*: knowing that Paris is the capital of France, or knowing that the word "chair" was presented in the previous list. Our memory for this form of knowledge usually takes the form of conscious recollection (e.g. "Ah yes, let me see now … I think that the capital of France is Paris"). This is not the only kind of knowledge that we possess.

A possible structure
for long-term memory.

Declarative Knowledge		Procedural Knowledge (e.g. motor skills)
Episodic memory (autobio-graphical)	**Semantic memory** (knowledge of the world)	

Most of us know how to ride a bicycle, but we would find it virtually impossible to describe what is involved in riding a bicycle. The term *procedural knowledge* is used to refer to *knowing how*: knowing how to type, knowing how to play tennis, and other skills that we have acquired. Memory for procedural knowledge is demonstrated by skilled performance (e.g. actually typing a document) rather than by saying what would be involved.

Failure to appreciate the distinction between declarative and procedural knowledge can produce many problems. For example, it is often assumed that outstanding football players will make successful coaches and managers because of the skills that they have acquired. This overlooks the fact that their skills involve primarily procedural knowledge, whereas teaching is mainly at the level of declarative knowledge.

During the course of skill acquisition, there is often an initial reliance on declarative learning followed by a switch to procedural learning. Typing illustrates this learning sequence. Initially there is the slow process of learning where each letter is and thinking about the positions of the letters (e.g. "F is the home key for the index finger on the left hand, and R is just above it"). Later on, the knowledge about letter positions is "in the fingertips", so much so that experienced typists often have to imagine typing a given letter in order to tell you where it is on the keyboard.

Strong evidence in support of the distinction between declarative and procedural knowledge has come from the study of amnesics suffering from Korsakoff's syndrome, a condition which results from chronic alcoholism. It was thought for a long time that these amnesics had practically no ability to form new long-term memories. They often cannot recall people they have met or events that have happened to them quite recently. They will even eat a meal despite the fact they had a large meal only an hour or so previously.

While these findings demonstrate that Korsakoff patients have greatly impaired declarative learning, they do not tell us anything about procedural learning. When procedural learning has been looked at, the results are quite dramatic. The patients' ability to learn a wide range of motor skills is as good as that of normal individuals. Even more remarkably, Korsakoff patients who have spent a long time developing a skill such as piano playing nevertheless often deny ever having seen the piano before as they arrive for each lesson. In other words, these amnesic patients have a virtually intact ability to store procedural knowledge in long-term memory combined with a marked inability to store declarative knowledge.

Long-term memory: explicit versus implicit

We have seen that long-term memory can be divided up into episodic and semantic memory or into procedural and declarative knowledge. It is also possible to distinguish between different kinds of long-term memory on the basis of the way in which memory is tested. Graf and Schachter (1985) argued that there is an important theoretical distinction between *explicit* and *implicit memory*, which they defined in the following way:

> Implicit memory is revealed when performance on a task is facilitated in the absence of conscious recollection; explicit memory is revealed when performance on a task requires conscious recollection of previous experiences. [p. 501]

Traditional measures of long-term memory such as free recall, cued recall, and recognition all involve the use of direct instructions to retrieve information about specific experiences, and are therefore measures of explicit memory.

Perhaps the main reason why psychologists have become interested in the distinction between explicit and implicit memory is because it appears to shed light on the memory problems of amnesic patients. Amnesic patients generally perform rather poorly when given tests of explicit memory, but often perform as well as normal individuals when given tests of implicit memory. An interesting experiment demonstrating this was reported by Graf, Squire, and Mandler (1984). They used three different tests of explicit memory for lists of words: free recall; cued recall, where the first three letters of each list word were given; and recognition. They also used a test of implicit memory: word completion. On the word-completion test, subjects were given three-letter word fragments (e.g. bar-) and simply had to write down the first word they thought of which started with those letters (e.g. barter, bargain). Implicit memory was assessed by the extent to which the word completions corresponded to words on the

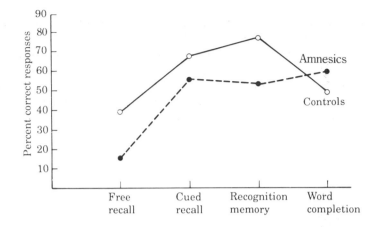

Free recall, cued recall, recognition memory, and word completion in amnesic patients and controls. Data from Graf, Squire and Mandler (1984).

list previously presented. As the figure above shows, the amnesic patients did much worse than control subjects on all the tests of explicit memory, but the two groups did not differ in their performance on the test of implicit memory.

There are several other studies in which amnesic patients showed good implicit memory but poor explicit memory. For example, Cohen (1984) made use of a game known as the Tower of Hanoi. The game involves five rings of different sizes and three pegs.

The rings are originally placed on the first peg with the largest one at the bottom and the smallest one at the top. The task is to produce the same arrangement of rings on the third peg. In order to achieve this, only one ring at a time can be moved, and a larger ring can never be placed on a smaller one. In spite of the complex nature of this task, Cohen (1984) discovered that amnesic patients found the best solution as rapidly as control subjects. However, there was a significant difference between the performance of the two groups when they were given a recognition test of explicit memory. On this test, they were presented with various arrangements of the rings. Some of these arrangements were taken from various stages of the task *en route* to the best solution. Others were not. The subjects had to decide which were which. The control subjects performed reasonably well on this test, whereas the performance of the amnesic patients was near to chance level. The fact that the amnesic patients performed well on the Tower of Hanoi task but showed poor conscious awareness of the steps involved in producing that performance suggests that their implicit memory was good but their explicit memory was not.

Memory research used to be based mainly on the assessment of explicit memory. It was therfore assumed that amnesic patients had very little ability to form new long-term memories. We now understand more fully that memory can be demonstrated by successful performance (implicit memory), regardless of whether or not there is conscious awareness of having acquired the relevant information in the past. While the distinction between explicit and implicit memory appears to be an important one in the light of amnesia research, it does suffer from some limitations. In particular, the distinction is descriptive rather than explanatory. Thus, for example, knowing that amnesic patients have good implicit memory but poor explicit memory is no more than the first step on the way to an explanation of amnesia, because the processes involved in implicit and explicit memory are not known.

Levels of processing

So far in this chapter we have focused on the multi-store approach to memory, and on subsequent theoretical modifications to the short-term and long-term stores which have been proposed by various theorists. Some theorists have gone even further, and disputed the whole notion of regarding human memory as divided up into boxes or stores. Among the most influential of these theorists were Fergus Craik and Robert Lockhart, who put forward their *levels-of-processing theory* in 1972. They argued that long-term memory traces are formed as a consequence of the processes that occur at the time of learning, and that memory theorists should accordingly focus on those processes. If, for example, you encounter the word "elephant", you might process information about the individual letters in the word, or its sound, or its meaning. Craik and Lockhart (1972) claimed that memory depends on the depth or level of processing, with deep processing involving processing of meaning. According to Craik and Lockhart (1972): "Trace persistence is a function of depth of analysis, with deeper levels of analysis associated with more elaborate, longer lasting, and stronger traces" (p. 675).

It seems reasonable to assume that we tend to remember things which are meaningful to us. As most students find, it is essential to understand thoroughly the meaning of what you are reading if you are going to be able to remember it later. There are several experimental studies which illustrate the point that it is important to process meaning. For example, Hyde and Jenkins (1973) set different groups of subjects to perform each of the following five processing tasks on words that were either associatively related or unrelated (in terms of meaning):

1. rating the words for pleasantness;
2. estimating the frequency of use of each word in English;

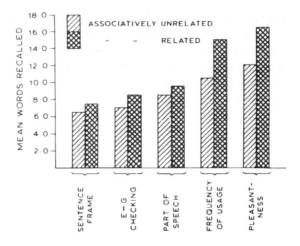

Mean words recalled as a function of list type (associatively related or unrelated) and orienting task. Data from Hyde and Jenkins (1973).

3. detecting the occurrence of the letters "e" and "g" in the list words;
4. deciding the part of speech (noun, verb, etc.) appropriate to each word;
5. deciding whether the list words fitted sentences containing blank spaces.

Hyde and Jenkins assumed that the first two tasks both involved the processing of meaning, whereas the other three tasks did not. They assessed long-term memory by means of a test of free recall shortly after the completion of the processing tasks.

The results are shown in the figure above. Free recall was 51% higher after tasks involving the processing of meaning for the list of associatively unrelated words; and 83% after semantic tasks for the list of associatively related words. In other words, the findings provide striking support for the levels-of-processing theory.

Craik and Lockhart (1972) were not only critical of the multi-store approach for its emphasis on the structure of human memory rather than on the processes involved in learning. They also felt that Atkinson and Shiffrin (1968) had provided an over-simplified view of rehearsal. According to Craik and Lockhart (1972), there are two different forms of rehearsal. Type 1, or maintenance rehearsal, involves a repetition of processes which have already been carried out (e.g. simply repeating a word over and over again). Type 2, or elaborative rehearsal, involves deeper processing of the stimulus material that is to be learned. It was claimed that Type 2 rehearsal improves long-term memory, while Type 1 rehearsal does not. The notion that there is a form of rehearsal that does not lead to enhanced learning is at odds with the multi-store theory, but makes some intuitive sense. If, for example, someone asked you to remember a string of words in a language you didn't know— say, Swedish—you would probably not remember the words a few hours later no matter how many times you had muttered them over to yourself via maintenance rehearsal.

In fact, the evidence provides a measure of comfort for both theoretical positions (see Eysenck, 1982b, for a detailed review). As the multi-store theory would predict, maintenance rehearsal usually leads to improved long-term memory. However, as the levels-of-processing theory predicts, maintenance or rote rehearsal generally improves memory much less than does elaborative rehearsal. The best solution may be to replace the clear-cut distinction between maintenance and elaborative rehearsal with a range of rehearsal activities ranging from mere rote or maintenance rehearsal to very elaborate rehearsal processes.

How should we evaluate the levels-of-processing theory? On the positive side, it is surely true that the specific processing activities occurring at the time of learning have a major impact on subsequent long-term memory. On the negative side, it is often rather difficult to ascertain what the depth of processing is in any particular case. Suppose we ask someone to decide what part of speech (e.g. noun, verb, adjective) each word in a list belongs to. Some psychologists argue that this task requires some attention to the meaning of each word and thus involves deep processing, whereas others have claimed that the part-of-speech task involves only shallow processing. The real problem is that there is no satisfactory measure of processing depth, and disagreements such as this cannot be resolved.

While depth of processing is important, there are other aspects of processing which play a part in determining long-term memory. Two such aspects are *elaboration* and *distinctiveness*. Elaboration refers to the amount of information that is processed at a particular level. If one person sees the word "clock" and thinks of the different materials and colours that clocks can be made in, and of specific clocks he or she knows, and of the dictionary definition of "clock", while a second person sees the same word but thinks only of its dictionary definition, then both people have engaged in deep processing. The first person has processed the word in a much more elaborate or extensive fashion, however, and will thus be more likely to remember the word later. It has also been discovered that memory traces which are distinctive or unique in some way are better remembered than those which are not distinctive (Eysenck, 1979). For example, a distinctive event, such a natural disaster, is easy to remember, because it stands out from our everyday memories. A systematic attempt to assess the relative importance of depth, elaboration, and distinctiveness in affecting long-term memory is now needed in this area of research. More of a theoretical understanding of *why* each of these three aspects of processing benefits memory is also required.

One final problem with levels-of-processing theory is the assumption that deep processing will always lead to better long-term memory than shallow processing. This assumption was disproved by Morris, Bransford, and Franks (1977). They argued that different kinds of processing lead learners to acquire different kinds of information about a stimulus. Whether the information stored as a result of performing a given processing task leads to subsequent retention depends upon the *relevance* of that information to the kind of memory test that is used. They tested this idea in an experiment where subjects had to answer semantic or shallow (rhyme) questions about words in a list. Memory was tested either by means of a standard recognition test, in which a mixture of list and non-list words was presented, or by a rhyming recognition test. On this latter test, subjects had to select words that rhymed with list words; the list words themselves were not presented. For example, if the word "whip" was on the rhyming test and the word "ship" had been in the list, subjects should have selected it because it rhymed with a list word.

Some of the findings are presented below. The predicted superiority of deep processing over shallow processing was found with the standard recognition test. However, the opposite result was obtained with the

Mean proportion of words recognised as a function of orienting task (semantic or rhyme) and of the type of recognition test (standard or rhyming).

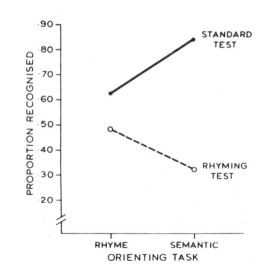

rhyme test, and this finding refutes the prediction of levels-of-processing theory that deep processing always leads to better long-term memory than shallow processing. The reason is that processing the meaning of the list words was essentially irrelevant when the memory test required the identification of words rhyming with list words. The information acquired from the shallow rhyme task was far more relevant, and so memory performance was higher in this condition.

Organisation in memory

One of the more important findings concerning human memory is that it is usually highly organised. Furthermore, the more organised the information in memory is, the better we are able to remember it. The existence of organisation in memory can be demonstrated in a very straightforward fashion. A categorised word list is prepared containing a number of words belonging to each of several different categories (e.g. four-footed animals, sports, flowers, articles of furniture, and so on). The list is then presented in a random order (e.g. tennis, cat, desk, golf, carnation, and so on), followed by a test of free recall in which the words can be written down in any order. The almost invariant finding is that the words are not recalled in a random order; instead, they tend to be recalled category by category. This phenomenon is known as *categorical clustering*, and it illustrates the way in which presented information is structured and organised by the knowledge stored in long-term memory (see Eysenck, 1977).

As you might expect, the degree of organisation present in recall differs from person to person. Some subjects recall entirely category-by-category, whereas others mix up the categories to some extent in their recall. A key finding is that those subjects who use categorical clustering the most tend to recall the greatest number of words. It is tempting to conclude that the extent of organisation determines the amount of recall. However, all we have here is basically a correlation between two measures (i.e. categorical clustering and recall), and it is inappropriate to infer causation from correlational evidence.

We have been considering what is known as experimenter-imposed organisation. That is to say, the experimenter deliberately selects a list of words having a certain organisational structure, and he or she then sees to what extent the subjects make use of that structure. An interesting question is whether organisational processes are so pervasive that they can be demonstrated with lists of words lacking any obvious structure at all. This issue was addressed by Mandler (1967). He simply presented his subjects with lists of words selected at random, and asked them to sort the words into a given number of categories (between two and seven). When the subjects had sorted the words in a consistent fashion, they were asked to recall as many of the words as possible.

Recall was poorest for those who had used two categories, and increased in a remarkably steady way by about four words per extra category used. Those who used seven categories recalled on average twenty words more than those who used only two. According to Mandler, the larger the number of categories that were used, the greater the amount of organisation imposed on the list. These findings can therefore be regarded as further evidence of the power of organisational processes to benefit memory. Since the list had no explicit structure, we are dealing here with subject-based organisation rather than experimenter-imposed organisation.

Organisational phenomena are by no means confined to memory for individual words. When people are presented with a lengthy passage to learn, their recall shows clear signs of being organised. In this case, the organisation involves taking account of the differential importance of the various ideas contained in the passage. The more important or theoretically relevant ideas tend to be recalled, whereas the less important ideas are ignored. What is recalled thus resembles closely a precis of the passage, which encapsulates the major themes. This was demonstrated most clearly by Gomulicki (1956). He asked one group of subjects to recall a passage they had seen previously, and he asked everyone in another group to write a precis of the same passage while it was in front of them. Further subjects were shown what these groups had written, and were unable to identify accurately the recalls from the precis.

Storage or retrieval?

Structure in recall may occur because the list words are organised at the time of learning or storage. An alternative possibility is that organisation is achieved at the time of retrieval (e.g. with category names being used to generate recall of the members of each category). In fact, there are effects occurring at storage and at retrieval. Very direct evidence that organisation is present during learning was obtained by Weist (1972). He used the conventional approach of presenting a categorised word list in a random order, followed by a test for free recall. However, he introduced the novel twist of asking the subjects to rehearse out loud during learning, and he took a tape recording of their overt rehearsal. There were two findings of interest:

- first, overt rehearsal showed clear evidence that organisation into categories occurs during learning; and

- second, the more organised the rehearsal was, the better the subjects's recall tended to be.

Endel Tulving and Zena Pearlstone (1966) had a look at retrieval. They presented lists of categorised words followed by free recall. After free recall, the subjects were presented with the category names as retrieval cues, and told to make a further attempt to recall the list words. The subjects were generally able to recall extra words when provided with the category names, and this was especially true when the list contained numerous categories. What probably happened was that people used the category names as cues to assist recall of the list words, but they were sometimes unable to remember all of the category names. Presenting the category names at the time of retrieval enabled the subjects to use their normal retrieval strategy in a more efficient way.

Categorised word lists are stored in a two-level hierarchy, with the category names at the top level of the hierarchy and members of each category at the bottom level. Memory limitations mean that it is difficult to remember more than a relatively small number of categories, and the same is true for members within categories. This line of thinking led Mandler (1967) to suggest that no more than five different items or clusters of items can be recalled from a single level of the hierarchy.

In general terms, the beneficial effects of organisation on memory are due to learners capitalising on relevant knowledge to make sense of the to-be-learned stimulus material. The powerful effects of relevant knowledge or expertise were demonstrated several years ago by De Groot (1966). He discovered that chess masters were much better than novice players at recalling actual board positions from chess games, but the two groups did not differ in their ability to memorise randomly arranged pieces. It is only in the former case that the chess masters could make full use of their vast knowledge of chess. The implication is that, if we are to arrive at a proper understanding of organisational phenomena, we must consider the underlying structure of semantic memory.

Semantic memory

Our permanent store of knowledge about language and about the world is often referred to as semantic memory. Despite the fact that semantic memory can contain millions of items of information, we are nevertheless able to answer most questions about that information extremely rapidly and with apparent ease. For example, we can decide in approximately one second that a sparrow is a bird, and it takes the same length of time to think of the name of a fruit starting with the letter "p". The great efficiency

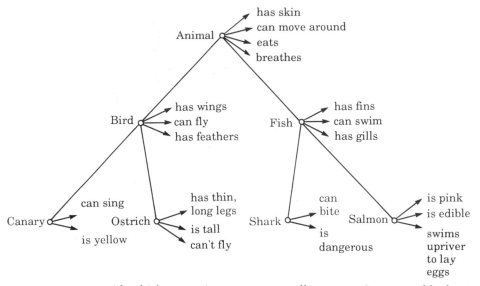

with which semantic memory normally operates is presumably due to the fact that it is highly organised or structured.

The first systematic theory of semantic memory was put forward by Allan Collins and Ross Quillian (1969). Their key assumption was that semantic memory is organised into a series of hierarchical networks. Part of one such hierarchical network is shown in the diagram above. The major concepts (e.g. animal, bird, canary) are represented as nodes, and there are properties or features (e.g. has wings, is yellow) associated with each concept. You may wonder why the property "can fly" is stored with the bird concept rather than with the canary concept: after all, one of the characteristics of canaries is that they can fly. According to Collins and Quillian (1969), it would waste space in semantic memory to have information about being able to fly stored with every bird name. If those properties which are possessed by nearly all birds (e.g. can fly, has wings) are stored only at the bird node or concept, this satisfies the notion of cognitive economy. The underlying principle is that property information is stored as high up the hierarchy as possible in order to minimise the amount of information that needs to be stored in semantic memory.

Collins and Quillian (1969) tested their theory by using a speeded verification task, in which subjects had to decide as quickly as possible whether sentences were true or false. It should be possible to decide very rapidly that the sentence, "A canary is yellow", is true, because the concept (i.e. "canary") and the property (i.e. "is yellow") are stored together at the same level of the hierarchy. In contrast, the sentence, "A canary can fly", should take longer, because the concept and the property are separated by one level in the hierarchy, and the sentence, "A canary has skin", should take even longer, because there are two levels separating the concept and the property. As predicted, the time taken to respond to true sentences became progressively slower as the separation between the subject of the sentence and the predicate became greater.

One of the attractive features of the theory proposed by Collins and Quillian (1969) is that its hierarchical structure provides a potential explanation for the hierarchical organisation observed in numerous memory experiments. The theory also seems to be on the right lines when it claims that we often use semantic memory successfully by *inferring* the right answer. For example, the information that Leonardo da Vinci had knees is not stored directly in our semantic memory. However, we do know that Leonardo da Vinci was a human being, and that human beings have knees, and so we can confidently infer that Leonardo da Vinci had knees. This is exactly the kind of inferential process proposed by Collins and Quillian (1969).

In spite of its successes, the theory suffers from a number of problems. As you may have noticed, a sentence such as, "A canary is yellow" differs from, "A canary has skin" not only in the hierarchical distance between the concept and its property, but also in familiarity. Indeed, you have probably never encountered the sentence, "A canary has skin", in your life before. Unfortunately for Collins and Quillian (1969), when the different sets of sentences are equated for familiarity, the number of levels separating concept and property has essentially no effect on verification time. There is another problem with their theory, relating to the prediction that the time required to decide that a member of a category does indeed belong to that category should be the same regardless of how typical or representative of that category the member actually is. Thus, for example, it should take no longer to decide that, "A chicken is a bird", is true than to make the same decision for, "A robin is a bird". In fact, verification times are faster for the more typical members of a category (e.g. robin).

Many of the problems with Collins and Quillian's (1969) network theory were sorted out by Collins and Loftus (1975) in their *spreading activation theory*. They argued that the notion of logically organised hierarchies was too inflexible and made little psychological sense. Instead, according to Collins and Loftus (1975), it is preferable to assume that semantic memory is organised on the basis of semantic relatedness or semantic distance. Semantic relatedness can be measured by asking people to decide how closely related pairs of words are. Alternatively, people can be asked to list as many members as they can of a particular category; those members produced most often are regarded as most closely related to the category.

According to spreading activation theory , whenever a person sees, hears, or thinks about a concept, the appropriate node in semantic memory is activated. The activation then spreads most strongly to other concepts which are closely related semantically, and more weakly to concepts which are more distant semantically. For example, activation would pass strongly from "robin" to "bird" in the sentence, "A robin is a bird", because "robin" and "bird" are closely related semantically, and this would help the subject to decide rapidly that the sentence is true.

The evidence indicates that semantic relatedness or distance is a very important determinant of speed of performance on the verification task. Among other findings which are handled neatly is one that we discussed earlier. This is the finding that the greater the semantic closeness of an instance and a category, the faster the decision that the instance is a member of that category.

Schemata

So far we have looked at ways in which words might be organised within the long-term memory system. It also seems probable that we possess much larger chunks of organised knowledge, and the term *schema* (plural *schemata*) to describe this was proposed by Sir Frederic Bartlett in 1932. He used the term in a rather vague way, but there has been subsequent agreement that a schema should be regarded as a mental representation that consists of a coherent collection of knowledge concerning a type of event, situation, or object. Other theorists have preferred the terms *script* or *frame* to schema to refer to organised structures of stereotypic knowledge.

The work of Bower, Black, and Turner (1979) serves to make concrete what is involved. They argued, for example, that most people have a restaurant script (or schema)—i.e. they have clear expectations about the sequence of events likely to take place during a meal at a restaurant. They tested this idea by asking 32 people to list the 20 most important events associated with having a meal at a restaurant. At least 73% of those questioned included the following six events in their list: sitting down; looking at the menu; ordering; eating; paying the bill; and leaving the restaurant. In addition, between 48% and 73% included the following nine events as part of their restaurant script or schema: entering the restaurant; giving the reservation name; ordering drinks; discussing the menu; talking; eating a salad or soup; ordering dessert; eating dessert; and leaving a tip. The restaurant script thus appears to be fairly uniform from one person to the next.

When we are reading a book or listening to what someone is saying, we frequently have to be actively involved in order to fill in the various gaps in the presented information. Consider the following short passage:

Fleur, Willie, and Juliet went to McArthur's restaurant in Wimbledon.
They enjoyed their chat together.
They left some money on the table.
They no longer felt hungry or tired.

This passage is quite easy to follow, but only because we use our restaurant script or schema to make sense of it. It is not actually stated that the money was left on the table deliberately as a tip, but that is what most people would assume. No reasons are explicitly provided to explain why Fleur, Willie, and Juliet no longer felt hungry or tired, but probably the food they ate at the restaurant eliminated their hunger, and sitting down throughout the meal restored their energy. This "gap filling" is more technically known as *inference drawing*, and it is one of the prime uses of scripts or schemata to allow inferences to be drawn in a way which is usually accurate and helpful for comprehension (see also Chapter 5).

We have just seen how schemata can influence the way in which we understand and make sense of information that is presented to us. According to Sir Frederic Bartlett (1932), memory is also affected by schemata. More specifically, he claimed that memory is determined in a complex fashion by the presented information and by relevant prior knowledge in the form of schemata.

How can we demonstrate the impact of schemata on memory? Bartlett came up with the ingenious idea of presenting people with stories that were in conflict with their knowledge of the world represented in schematic form. He achieved this in his most famous study by testing the ability of English subjects to remember a story they had read called *The War of the Ghosts*, which comes from the North American Indian culture. Bartlett predicted that the subjects" stored schemata would produce systematic distortions in their recall of the story, eliminating some of the peculiarities of the original. You might find it interesting to read it, and then to write down as much as you can remember of the story afterwards.

The War of the Ghosts
One night two young men from Egulac went down to the river to hunt seals and while they were there it became foggy and calm. Then they heard war-cries, and they thought, "Maybe this is a war-party." They escaped to the shore, and hid behind a log. Now canoes came up, and they heard the noise of paddles, and saw one canoe coming up to them. There were five men in the canoe, and they said, "What do you think? We wish to take you along. We are going up the river to make war on the people." One of the young men said, "I have no arrows." "Arrows are in the canoe," they said.

"I will not go along. I might be killed. My relatives do not know where I have gone. But you," he said, turning to the other, "may go with them." So one of the young men went, but the other returned home. And the warriors went on up the river to a town on the other side of Kalama. The people came down to the water, and they began to fight, and many were killed. But presently the young man heard one of the warriors say, "Quick, let us go home; that Indian has been hit." Now he thought, "Oh, they are ghosts." He did not feel sick, but they said he had been shot. So the canoes went back to Egulac, and the young man went ashore to his house, and made a fire. And he told everybody and said, "Behold I accompanied the ghosts, and we went to fight. Many of our fellows were killed, and many of those who attacked us were killed. They said I was hit, and I did not feel sick." He told it all, and then he became quiet. When the sun rose he fell down. Something black came out of his mouth. His face became contorted. The people jumped up and cried. He was dead.

How did your recall differ from the original story? Bartlett found that most of the mistakes his subjects made in recalling the story had the effect of making it read more like a conventional English story. For example, one subject wrote that a dying Indian "foamed at the mouth", whereas the orignal tale contains the phrase, "something black came out of his mouth". Bartlett described this kind of memorial distortion as *rationalisation*. He also identified other systematic errors in recall, including *flattening* (i.e. a failure to remember unfamiliar details) and *sharpening* (i.e. elaborating on some of the details contained in the story).

There are two major problems with Bartlett's research at an experimental level. First, it is possible that some of the distortions produced by his subjects were not really due to faulty memory, but rather were a more or less deliberate attempt to produce a coherent recall. Indeed, when subjects are instructed that they must strive to avoid all inaccuracies in their recall, then almost half of the errors found by Bartlett disappear (Gauld & Stephenson, 1967). The fact that a majority of the errors remain, however, indicates that many of the distortions in recall are genuine failures of memory. Secondly, it has been argued that Bartlett's work is of little general interest because he had to resort to stories from an unfamiliar culture in order to obtain evidence for schemata. However, studies carried out by John Bransford and his colleagues (reported in Bransford, 1979) indicate that Bartlett-type effects can be found with very ordinary material. Bransford presented his subjects with simple stories (e.g. "When the man entered the kitchen, he slipped on a wet spot and dropped the delicate glass pitcher on the floor. The pitcher was very expensive, and everyone watched the event with horror"). On a subsequent recognition-memory test, the subjects were very likely to say that they had heard the sentence, "When the man entered the kitchen, he slipped on a wet spot and broke the delicate glass pitcher when it fell on the floor". Presumably their schematic knowledge about pitchers encouraged them to draw the reasonable inference that the pitcher broke, and this led to errors in recognition memory.

At the theoretical level, Bartlett (1932) seems to have believed that memorial distortions occur largely through schemata affecting the retrieval process. He argued that retrieval is a process of reconstruction, and schemata are involved in this process. While this is sometimes true, it seems more likely that schemata usually produce distorted memory through their influence on the ways in which the stimulus material is understood at the time of learning. This issue is dealt with at greater length in Chapter 5.

There is a further theoretical problem with many of the schema-based theories of memory. Such theories often provide insightful accounts of the reasons why memory is inaccurate and distorted, but they go too far in the direction of claiming that memory is usually inaccurate. We often remember fairly precisely personal remarks that other people make about us, and actors and actresses must of necessity remember their parts with perfect accuracy. Such phenomena are not easily incorporated into schema theory, with its emphasis on the ways in which schemata alter what is presented in systematic ways.

Why do we forget?

One of the most interesting aspects of memory is forgetting. Many people complain that they have a very poor memory and are always forgetting things such as people's names, wedding anniversaries, or the punch lines of jokes. This complaint is unfair to our memory systems, because memory can perform many impressive feats that we take for granted. For example, despite the very large number of words stored in long-term memory, you could probably decide in approximately one second that "edifice" is a word in the English language, and you could decide with equal speed that "mantiness" is not.

It is true, of course, that we do forget many things we desperately want to remember, and common sense suggests that there are all sorts of reasons for forgetting. However, we can make a start by noting that there are basically only two major reasons for forgetting. Endel Tulving (1974) described these reasons as *trace-dependent forgetting* and *cue-dependent forgetting*. As the term implies, trace-dependent forgetting occurs because the memory trace has deteriorated or decayed, and has consequently been

"WHAT BOTHERS ME, IS HOW WILL I KNOW WHEN I *HAVE* FORGOTTEN EVERYTHING?"

lost from the memory system. Cue-dependent forgetting means that the information is still stored in long-term memory, but there is no suitable retrieval cue to trigger off the memory. Cue-dependent forgetting can be illustrated by the fact that most people find that their recollections of childhood become fainter as they grow older. However, if they return to the area they lived in as children, the streets, houses, and school often serve to bring the past alive. In other words, the physical environment of childhood can act as an effective cue proving that many memory traces established a long time ago are not eliminated from the memory system.

Permanent memory

Many psychologists have been sufficiently impressed by the evidence in favour of cue-dependent forgetting to argue that all forgetting is of this type. That is to say, there is permanent storage of information and forgetting occurs solely as a result of using inappropriate retrieval cues. Loftus and Loftus (1980) discovered that 84% of psychologists believed in the notion of permanent storage, and so did 69% of non-psychologists. Advocates of the permanent memory hypothesis often cite as evidence either the work of Wilder Penfield or the power of hypnosis to recover previously forgotten memories.

Penfield (1969) operated on a large number of epileptic patients. During the course of his work, he frequently stimulated the surface of the brain with a rather weak electric current in order to identify the area of the brain involved in epilepsy. Quite by chance, he discovered that some of his patients seemed to relive events from their past with great vividness when the electrode stimulated certain parts of the brain. Penfield (1969) was in no doubt about the significance of his findings:

> It is clear that the neuronal action that accompanies each succeeding state of consciousness leaves its permanent imprint on the brain. The imprint, or record, is a trail of facilitation of neural connections that can be followed again by an electric current many years later with no loss of detail, as though a tape recorder had been receiving it all. [p. 165].

In fact, the evidence does not really support this conclusion. A total of 520 epileptic patients received electrical stimulation of the cortex, but only 40 of them reported the recovery of long-lost memories. While Penfield claimed that the patients' recollections were very vivid and detailed, in most cases they were actually somewhat vague and limited to just one sense modality (usually visual or auditory). A further problem is that Penfield had no independent verification of his patients' recollections, and some of them may not have been genuine memories at all. We must conclude that the permanent memory hypothesis receives no more than modest support from the research of Wilder Penfield.

What about work on hypnosis? Police forces in several countries make use of hypnosis with eyewitnesses in order to improve their memory for events surrounding crimes. Some difficulties with the use of hypnosis were uncovered by Putnam (1979). He showed his subjects a videotape in which a car and a bicycle were involved in an accident. Those subjects who were subsequently questioned about the accident while hypnotised made significantly more mistakes in their answers than did those who responded in the non-hypnotised state.

What appears to happen is that hypnosis makes people less cautious in reporting their memories than they would normally be. This lack of caution may sometimes lead to the recovery of previously inaccessible memories, but it also produces many inaccurate memories. Perhaps the clearest illustration of this is that hypnotised people will often "recall" events from the future with great confidence.

In view of the evidence, it is surprising that the permanent memory hypothesis remains popular. Part of the reason for its popularity is that none of the evidence produced in this field disproves the hypothesis. We must accept the possibility that information is stored somewhere in long-term memory even if it proves impossible to retrieve it by the use of hypnosis or other techniques. We must also admit that much (or even most) forgetting is cue-dependent rather than trace-dependent. However, the fact that there is no compelling evidence at all in favour of the permanent memory hypothesis indicates that we should be careful about aligning ourselves with the 84% of psychologists who agree with it.

Cue-dependent forgetting

While the permanent memory hypothesis assumes that all forgetting is cue-dependent forgetting, it does not indicate *why* it is that some cues fail to elicit particular memories, nor does it tell us how cue-dependent forgetting actually occurs. An attempt to do just that was made by Endel Tulving and Zena Pearlstone (1966) in the study mentioned earlier in the chapter. First of all, they established that cue-dependent forgetting can be very extensive. Long lists of words belonging to several different categories (e.g., articles of furniture; four-footed animals) were presented. Subjects were then asked to write down as many of the words as they could remember (non-cued recall); after that, they were given all of the category names as cues and again asked to write down the list words (cued recall). They discovered that subjects could remember up to three or four times as many words under cued recall as they could under non-cued recall. The relatively poor performance under non-cued recall occurred because the helpful cues presented in cued recall were absent—i.e. there was a substantial amount of cue-dependent forgetting.

In his subsequent research and theorising, Endel Tulving has argued that whether a retrieval cue leads to remembering or not depends critically on the extent to which the information in the cue matches or "fits" the information contained in the memory trace. Thus, for example, the retrieval cue, "What was the name of the woman in the yellow dress who was at the party last Saturday?", is unlikely to produce the correct answer unless the appropriate information about dress colour is actually stored in long-term memory. These notions about the importance of the information contained in the retrieval cue and in the memory trace were encapsulated by Tulving (1979) in his *encoding specificity principle*: "The probability of successful retrieval of the target item is a monotonically increasing function of informational overlap between the information present at retrieval and the information stored in memory" (p. 408). In simpler terms, the greater the similarity between the information contained in the retrieval cue and that contained in the memory trace, the higher the probability that the individual will remember the information he or she is seeking.

The most dramatic evidence supporting the encoding specificity principle comes from studies in which recall (i.e. remembering the name of something) is compared with recognition (i.e. deciding whether what is presented is exactly the same as what was learned initially). Common sense indicates that recognition should be superior to recall, and that is indeed the typical finding. According to the encoding specificity principle, this is because the informational overlap is usually much greater in the case of recognition tests than recall tests. However, it should theoretically be possible to make recall superior to recognition, provided that we maximise informational overlap for recall and minimise it for recognition.

This strategy was followed by Michael Watkins (1974). He asked people to learn pairs of items such as "SPANI" paired with "EL", and "EXPLO" paired with "RE". Of course, what they stored in long-term memory were the words "SPANIEL" and "EXPLORE". The second member of each pair (i.e. "EL"; "RE") was then tested by means of recognition tests (e.g., Do you recognise EL? RE?) and recall tests (e.g., What went with "SPANI"? "EXPLO"?). The result was that 67% of the items were recalled against only 9% recognised. The reason (according to the encoding specificity principle) is that the retrieval cues used in recall (i.e. "SPANI"; "EXPLO") had more informational overlap than the retrieval cues used in recognition (e.g., "EL"; "RE") with the relevant memory traces (e.g., "SPANIEL"; "EXPLORE").

Are there any problems with the encoding specificity principle? Perhaps the most obvious one is that it is rather difficult to test. We usually do not really know what information is stored in the memory trace or extracted from the retrieval cue, and so any assessment of the "informational overlap" between them is rather speculative. A second limitation is that when you try to remember something you can make use of a variety of different strategies. If, for example, you were asked what you did last Wednesday evening, then you might use a complex chain of thinking to find the answer (e.g., "Let's see, on Wednesday I usually play badminton, but last week was half-term, and so I arranged to go to Lord's with a friend"). This sort of problem-solving approach to memory retrieval is very common, but the encoding specificity principle tells us nothing about it.

Repression

Probably the best known theory of forgetting was advanced by Sigmund Freud, the controversial founder of the psychoanalytic movement. He argued that much forgetting occurs as a result of repression. It is generally assumed that by repression he meant motivated forgetting, in which the anxiety associated with a memory is so great that the memory is kept out of consciousness although it still exists in the unconscious mind. In fact, Freud actually used the term "repression" in a number of different ways. For example, he sometimes defined repression as the inhibition of the capacity for emotional experience. According to this definition, repression can occur even when there is conscious awareness of unpleasant memories, provided that these memories are deprived of their usual emotional content.

There are real problems associated with testing Freud's theory of repression. Proper experimental methods cannot be used in clinical settings. Such methods can, of course, be used in the laboratory, but for ethical reasons it is impossible to make use of the anxiety-producing and traumatic events involved in repression.

For what they are worth, experimental attempts to demonstrate the phenomenon of repression typically involve creating anxiety to produce forgetting or repression. After that the anxiety is removed to show that the repressed information is still in long-term memory (this is known as "return of the repressed"). More specifically, failure feed-back (telling subjects that their performance of a task is inadequate) has usually been used to produce anxiety, and then anxiety has been removed by reassuring the subjects that the failure feedback was false and that their performance was actually quite good.

Simply being told that one's performance of a task is poor is very different from the traumatic events that clinical patients have experienced. In spite of this, some evidence for repression and for the return of the repressed has been been obtained (see Eysenck and Keane, 1990). However, while failure feedback leads to impaired memory, it is not clear that repression is responsible. Another possibility is that the subjects think about their failure and the reasons for it rather than putting all of their efforts into the memory test. This explanation seems quite likely given the further finding (Holmes, 1972) that success feedback reduces recall as much as failure feedback: experiencing success can hardly cause repression, but might well divert attention from the recall task.

All in all, there is a lack of strong support for Freud's repression hypothesis. However, the plentiful anecdotal evidence emerging from clinical settings means that we should probably keep an open mind on the issue of whether the phenomenon of repression actually exists.

Interference

If you had asked psychologists what caused forgetting at any time during the 1930s, 1940s, or 1950s, you would probably have received the answer, "Interference". It was assumed that our subsequent memory for what we are currently learning may be disrupted or interfered with by what we have previously learned or by what we learn in the future. When previous learning interferes with later learning and retention, this is known as *proactive interference*, and when later learning disrupts earlier learning we have *retroactive interference*.

"THE TIME? YES, OF COURSE,...HERE,...NOPE,..TRY AGAIN,... A·HA·HA..LETS SEE..."

Suppose, for example, that you learn French first and then German. You will then have acquired two different foreign words to refer to each English word (e.g., "the boat" is "le bateau" or "das Schiff"). According to interference theory, learning German might interfere with your memory for French via retroactive interference, or your knowledge of French might impair you memory for German via proactive interference.

Interference theory can be traced back to the nineteenth century, and to a German psychologist called Hugo Munsterberg. That was the era of pocket-watches, and Munsterberg kept his watch in one particular pocket. When he started keeping it in a different pocket, he discovered that he was often fumbling about in confusion when asked for the time.

This anecdote illustrates the essence of interference theory. Munsterberg had learned an association between the stimulus "What time is it?" and the response of removing the watch from his pocket. Later on, the stimulus remained the same, but a different response was now associated with it (that is, the watch had to be removed from a different pocket). As a general rule of thumb, both proactive and retroactive interference tend to be maximal when two different responses have been associated with the same stimulus, intermediate when two similar stimuli are involved, and minimal when two dissimilar stimuli are involved.

Since proactive and retroactive interference have both been demonstrated countless times, why is it that interference theory no longer enjoys the popularity that it once did? There are two particularly important reasons. First, interference theory has rather little to say about the internal processes actually involved in learning and memory, whereas the central interest of cognitive psychology is in these processes. Second, it requires special circumstances for substantial interference effects to occur (i.e., the

	Proactive interference		
Group	Learn	Learn	Test
Experimental	A–B	A–C	A–C
	(e.g. Cat–Tree)	(e.g. Cat–Dirt)	(e.g. Cat–Dirt)
Control	—	A–C	A–C
		(e.g. Cat–Dirt)	(e.g. Cat–Dirt)

	Retroactive interference		
Group	Learn	Learn	Test
Experimental	A–B	A–C	A–B
	(e.g. Cat–Tree)	(e.g. Cat–Dirt)	(e.g. Cat–Tree)
Control	A–B	—	A–B
	(e.g. Cat–Tree)		(e.g. Cat–Tree)

Note: for both proactive and retroactive interference, the experimental group exhibits interference. On the test, only the first word is supplied, and the subjects must provide the second word.

same stimulus paired with two different responses), and these circumstances seem relatively rare in everyday life. In fact, probably only a small fraction of forgetting can be attributed to proactive and retroactive interference.

Practical applications

Most of the research we have discussed in this chapter has been concerned with memory under laboratory conditions. If we want to understand how memory functions in everyday life, it might seem that the obvious solution is to study memory in naturalistic settings. However, this approach has its own limitations, in particular the difficulty of establishing proper experimental control. While we can often measure accurately how much an individual remembers about a specific event or person, information about the time and extent of learning is usually lacking. For example, it was found that practically no one could locate correctly all of the letters and numbers on the British telephone dials which were in general use until the early 1980s. This was a striking finding in view of the large number of times that most people were exposed to such dials. Any attempt to provide a comprehensive explanation for this poor memory performance is hampered by our lack of knowledge of exactly how people process information about letters and numbers while they are dialling a telephone number.

Studies of everyday memory have produced many intriguing and novel findings, and have served to highlight some of the major limitations of the laboratory approach. For example, laboratory research into memory has focused almost exclusively on *retrospective memory*, i.e. the ability to remember some event from the past. Everyday memory, however, often makes use of *prospective memory*, in which we need to remember to do things at specified times (e.g. we may have to take pills at certain times of day or we may have arranged to meet someone at a particular time). There is some evidence that prospective memory does not operate like retrospective memory. Wilkins and Baddeley (1978) found that those who did well on a test of prospective memory (remembering to press a button at previously specified times) tended to perform poorly on a test of retrospective memory (free recall of words). Retrospective memory generally declines over time, but Wilkins (1976) found that prospective memory (remembering to post a card) was as good when subjects were told to do this in 36 days' time as when they were instructed to do it in two days' time.

It is probably true to say that the greatest contribution of the everyday memory approach has been to present laboratory researchers with major new challenges and phenomena. The way in which the whole field of prospective memory has been opened up by researchers on everyday memory is a clear illustration of this point.

Remembering medical information

The study of everyday memory is still in its infancy, but already it has some success stories to its credit. A case in point concerns the important practical problem of patients forgetting much of the information provided by their doctors. Indeed, the patients' forgetting is so profound that many of them complain unjustifiably that their doctors have withheld relevant information from them.

Memory for medical information was investigated by Ley (1978). His first task was to discover which items of information were well remembered, and which were poorly remembered. Most of his findings were predictable from earlier laboratory studies. The initial information given by the doctor was well remembered (this has been found in free recall studies and is called the "primacy effect"), and the items rated most important by the patients were recalled better than those rated least important. Information which was organised into categories (e.g., medicines to take) was remembered better than unorganised information. Patients with more medical knowledge tended to remember more of what the doctor said than did the less knowledgeable, presumably because they found it easier to engage in elaborative processing. As would be expected by psychologists (but perhaps not by medical doctors), simply repeating information had rather little impact on the amount recalled.

Having established that memory for medical information in everyday settings obeyed essentially the same principles as memory for other kinds of information in the laboratory, Ley and his colleagues then prepared a booklet for medical practitioners in which they used their findings to provide suggestions for improved communication. Before the general practitioners received the booklet, their patients recalled approximately 55% of what they said; afterwards, that figure increased to 70%.

Mnemonic techniques

Of all the practical applications of memory research, the provision of techniques for improving memory would be of greatest use. Such mnemonic techniques (i.e. techniques designed to aid memory) have been developed, and have a lengthy history going back to the ancient Greeks. They invented the *method of loci* (i.e. the method of locations), which enables people to remember a large number of items in the correct order. The first step in this method is to memorise a series of locations, such as places along a familiar walk. After that, mental imagery is used to associate each of the items in turn with a specific location. When the individual then wants to recall the items, he or she carries out a "mental walk", simply recalling what is stored at each location along the walk. For example, you could remember the items that needed to be bought at the shops by imagining each item at different places along the walk—a loaf of bread at the park entrance and so on.

The method of loci is basically a peg system, in which the items that have to be remembered are associated with convenient pegs (e.g. locations on a walk). A more recent peg system is the one based on the rhyme:

one is a bun,	six is sticks,
two is a shoe,	seven is heaven,
three is a tree,	eight is a gate,
four is a door,	nine is a mine,
five is a hive,	ten is a hen.

Mental imagery is used to associate the first item that must be remembered with a bun, the second item with a shoe, and so on. The advantage of this version of the peg system is that you can rapidly produce any specific item in the series (e.g. the fifth or the eighth).

Why are the peg systems effective in enhancing memory? First, they provide a useful organisational structure. Secondly, the pegs act as powerful retrieval cues, and thus tend to prevent cue-dependent forgetting from occurring. Thirdly, the use of imagery has been found to increase learning in other situations.

There are other mnemonic techniques which attempt to impose organisation and meaning on the learning material. For example, the difficult business of remembering someone's name can be greatly facilitated in the following way. First of all, you change the person's name slightly into something which you can imagine (e.g. Eysenck might become "ice sink"). Then you choose a distinctive feature of that person's face, and associate the image with that feature (e.g. the nose might be thought of as a tap over the sink). In one study (Morris, Jones, and Hampson, 1978), the use of this technique improved people's ability to put names to faces by approximately 80%.

In spite of the successes of the various mnemonic techniques, they are rather limited in a number of ways. While they may allow us to remember long lists of unrelated items, they may not help us much with the complex learning required to pass examinations or to remember the contents of a book. It is certainly true that most mnemonic techniques do not lead to

increased understanding of the learning material. However, they are of considerable usefulness under certain circumstances (e.g. a harassed teacher trying to remember the names of the 30 or so pupils in his or her class).

The task of learning and remembering relatively long and complicated material can be eased by the use of a method of study known as SQ3R, which stands for Survey, Question, Read, Recite, Review. The SQ3R method of study works in practice and seems in accord with sound psychological principles (see Morris, 1979, for a review). It involves the learner actively, rather than passively, in the learning process. It also helps the integration of the learner's previous knowledge with the information contained in the text.

Summary: Memory

- An understanding of the functioning of human memory is of vital significance in the study of cognition because no cognitive processes could be carried out normally without a memory system.
- Storage of information can be looked at in various ways. Multi-store theorists argued that information proceeds through modality-specific stores and the short-term store before finally reaching the long-term store. This theoretical approach is rather over-simplified. The short-term store is better regarded as a multi-component working memory. The long-term store is not really homogeneous: we need to distinguish between episodic and semantic long-term memories, and between stores for proce-dural and for declarative knowledge. It is also important to distinguish between explicit and implicit memory, which differ in terms of whether or not there is conscious recollection of what is being remembered.
- Storage can also be thought of in terms of the kinds of processing which are most useful for long-term memory. This approach was adopted in the levels-of-processing theory. According to this theory, the deeper or more meaningful the processing of a stimulus is, the better will be its long-term retention.
- When considering storage, it is important to note that long-term memory is highly organised. In order for learning material to be well remembered, it must capitalise on the existing organisation of the long-term memory system.

- Retrieval of information from long-term memory depends on many factors. Of particular importance is the extent to which the information contained in the retrieval cue matches the information stored in long-term memory. This notion is encapsulated in Tulving's encoding specificity principle. Other important factors are the extent of decay of the memory trace, proactive and retroactive interference, and possibly repression.
- There have so far only been limited attempts to make memory research of practical relevance. However, the application of well-known laboratory principles to the issue of remembering medical information has proved reasonably successful. In addition, mnemonic techniques based on the peg system have been useful when long lists of unrelated items need to be remembered, and study methods have increased understanding and memory for complex texts.

Further reading

Cohen, G. (1989), *Memory in the Real World* (Hove, U.K.: Lawrence Erlbaum Associates Ltd.) provides a very readable account of research on everyday memory. Eysenck, M. W. and Keane, M. (1990), *Cognitive Psychology: A Student's Handbook*. Hove, U.K.: Lawrence Erlbaum Associates Ltd.) provide additional coverage of nearly all of the topics dealt with in this chapter.

5 Language comprehension and production

Given the tremendous importance of language in human existence, it is rather surprising that during the first 50 years or so of experimental psychology, most psychologists studiously avoided a systematic examination of language. How can this neglect be accounted for? Part of the answer may be, quite simply, that language is much harder to study than, for example, simple conditioned responses. A more important reason, however, is that the Behaviourist approach which held sway during that period was not well suited to explaining the psychology of language. Skinnerian *reinforcement theory* predicts that children will learn to say things which are followed by reward or reinforcement. Since it has been found (Brown, Cazden, & Bellugi, 1969) that middle-class American parents reinforce their children's speech primarily on the basis of its truth rather than on its grammatical accuracy, reinforcement theory would predict that these children would grow up speaking truthfully but ungrammatically. In fact, the opposite is closer to what actually happens—most adults speak reasonably grammatically but by no means always truthfully.

Progress in the study of language became more rapid following the linguistic analysis of language provided by Noam Chomsky (1957; 1965). He proposed a transformational grammar, which distinguished between the *syntax*, *phonology*, and *semantics* of language. Syntax deals with the rules specifying which strings of words are well formed and acceptable within the language. Phonology is concerned with the rules for moving from the phrases comprising a sentence to the appropriate sounds. The third component of the system, the semantics, contains the rules which determine the assignment of meaning to well-formed sentences.

Perhaps the best known of the theoretical distinctions put forward by Chomsky is that between the *surface structure* and the *deep structure* of a sentence. The surface structure divides a sentence into phrases. Thus, for example, the sentence, "They are cooking apples", has two different surface-structure representations. In one representation, "cooking" and "apples" belong to the same phrase (i.e. the sentence concerns a given type of apple—a cooking apple). In the other representation "cooking" belongs to the verb phrase (i.e. apples are being cooked). There are, however, some ambiguous sentences which cannot be resolved by considering the surface structure. For example, the surface or phrase structure of the following sentence is the same regardless of which interpretation is intended: "The police were ordered to stop drinking at midnight." In order to handle such problems, Chomsky argued that one needs to consider the deep structure, which reflects the meaning of a sentence more closely than does the surface structure. According to Chomsky, there are two deep structures associated with the sentence about the police, each one corresponding to a different interpretation of the sentence.

The notion of a deep structure is also useful in other ways. For example, the two sentences, "John hit Mary", and, "Mary was hit by John", have virtually the same meaning. This similarity in meaning is captured by the fact that both sentences have the same deep structure. The notion of a deep structure plays a central role in Chomsky's theoretical formulation. Both the meaning assigned to a sentence (i.e. the semantics) and the phonology of a sentence follow, and are based on, its deep-structure representation.

Chomsky's views on language were enormously influential within psychology during the late 1950s and early 1960s, but they have lost favour in the years since then. There are three main reasons for this:

- First, Chomsky was a linguist and not a psychologist, and he was much more interested in language itself than in the psychological processes of the language user.
- Second, Chomsky was mainly concerned with the syntax of language (both surface and deep-structure representations occur within the syntax component), whereas psychologists generally feel that meaning is of more importance than syntax or grammar.
- Third, Chomsky largely adopted the linguist's approach of considering sentences in isolation from the context in which they are spoken or read.

Some of the limitations of such an approach will become clear later in the chapter, but for now we can perhaps consider an example provided by Eysenck (1984). The meaning that we assign to the sentence, "I am not a crook", is likely to be different if spoken by the Archbishop of Canterbury than by ex-US President, Richard Nixon.

The contemporary approach to language adopted by cognitive psychologists is discussed in the sections which follow. Whereas Chomsky focused mainly on *linguistic competence* (i.e. the abstract knowledge that people possess about language), cognitive psychologists are interested in *linguistic performance* (i.e. actual language behaviour), and with the kinds of mistake that people make when understanding and producing language. The crucial difference between the two approaches is that cognitive psychologists want to understand the processes involved in language use, whereas Chomsky had very little to say on the subject.

It usually appears to be a relatively effortless matter to make sense of what we are reading or listening to in a conversation. However, there are actually numerous processes involved in comprehension. These include letter and word identification in reading or basic speech perception when listening, decisions about "what goes with what" in the stimulus input, and the extraction of meaning. In general terms, reading and speech perception differ most in terms of some of the initial stages of processing. For example, it is usually the case that speech provides considerably less clear information than printed text. Lieberman (1963) discovered that words in spoken sentences which were taped and then presented on their own could be recognised on only about 50% of occasions, which compares with about 100% accuracy for written words presented on their own.

The chapter begins by considering some of the processes that are specific to reading or to speech perception, and then focuses on the comprehension processes common to both.

Basic processes in reading

Eye movements

A useful way of investigating some of the processes involved in reading is to study the eye movements of people reading (see Rayner & Pollatsek, 1987 for a review). While we feel that our eyes move smoothly across a page of text, the reality is quite different. Our eyes actually make a series of rapid movements known as *saccades*, and between saccades there are fixation periods lasting for approximately 250 milliseconds. A point towards the beginning of a word is usually fixated, and there is a distance of approximately eight letters or spaces between successive fixations. While most fixations typically move forwards in the text, around 10 or 15% of them involve the eyes fixating an earlier part of the text than the previous fixation. Of particular importance, information is obtained from the text only during fixations and not at all during saccades. For example, Latour (1962) found that a bright flash of light which was presented only during a saccade was not seen.

The perceptual span.   How much information is extracted from a single fixation? Rayner and Pollatsek (1987) discuss various methods which have been used to measure what is known as the *perceptual span*, which is the range of letters from which useful information is extracted.

Not surprisingly, the perceptual span varies depending on factors such as the size of the print, the complexity of the text, and so on. It is typically the case, however, that the perceptual span encompasses about three or four letters to the left of fixation and some fifteen letters to the right of fixation. The opposite pattern is found in readers of Hebrew, who read from right to left. What appears to be happening is that it is more valuable to look ahead in the text rather than to look backwards to words which have already been processed.

The fact that the perceptual span covers almost 20 letters means that some of the letters included in it do not fall within the foveal region of the eye (see Chapter 2), which is the area of high acuity. What information is extracted from the area lying outside the fovea? Fairly complex studies have revealed that meaning is not extracted, but that information about the identity of the letters is obtained.

The immediacy assumption.   At what point is meaning extracted from the words in a text? According to Beck and Carpenter (1986), the reader carries out the processes required to understand each word and its relationship to previous words in the sentence as soon as that word is encountered; this is known as the *immediacy assumption*.

Carpenter and Daneman (1981) obtained some evidence consistent with the immediacy assumption. They included the following two sentences in an account of a fishing contest:

> Tomorrow was the annual, one-day fishing contest and fish-
> ermen would invade the place. Some of the best bass guitarists
> in the country would come to this spot.

These sentences were written specifically to confuse the subjects. It is natural to interpret "bass" as referring to a kind of fish, but the following word "guitarists" makes it clear that the appropriate meaning of "bass" is its musical one. Most readers fixated an unusually long time on the word "guitarists", which suggests that the ambiguity and its resolution were noticed almost immediately.

There is other evidence which indicates that the immediacy assumption is over-simplified. The fact that most readers sometimes move their eyes back to earlier parts of a text suggests that the meaning of text is not always extracted immediately. In addition, readers sometimes fixate the same word more than once, which is contrary to the spirit of the immediacy assumption.

Reading aloud

For most adults, the task of reading words aloud appears very straightforward, and the same would be true if you were asked to read aloud non-words such as "fint" or "mantiness". The task is a very straightforward one from the reader's point of view, but it poses some interesting theoretical complexities to cognitive psychologists. It is clear that there are various different processes that can be used to say printed words and non-words. For example, there are numerous words in the English language which have irregular spelling-sound correspondences—that is, they are not pronounced in predictable ways. Examples are "yacht", "pint", and "comb". Because it is impossible to guess how they should be pronounced, our ability to pronounce them correctly presumably depends on specific information about these words stored in long-term memory. With non-words like "fint" or "mantiness", on the other hand, there is no relevant information stored in memory. Accordingly, non-words are pronounced either on the basis of rules indicating the relationship between letter strings and sounds (sometimes called *grapheme-phoneme conversion rules*), or by analogy with real words (e.g. "fint" is pronounced to rhyme with "dint" and "mint"). Regular words (i.e. those which conform to grapheme-phoneme conversion rules) could be spoken accurately either on the basis of the conversion rules or on the basis of specific information about them stored in long-term memory.

Cognitive neuropsychologists have used some of these ideas to suggest that there may be three different routes between the printed word and its pronunciation (see the figure opposite for further details):

- Route 1. This route relies on pronouncing unfamiliar words or non-words by means of grapheme-phoneme conversion or by analogy with words whose pronunciation is known. This route is successful with words having regular spelling-sound correspondences and with non-words.
- Route 2. This route involves accessing the meaning of the written word and then its pronunciation from long-term memory. This route can be used only with familiar words.
- Route 3. This route also involves accessing the pronunciation of written words from long-term memory. Unlike Route 2, however, word meaning is not accessed, so that the written words that are pronounced are not understood.

Research on brain-damaged patients by cognitive neuropsychologists has provided reasonably strong support for this three-route model of

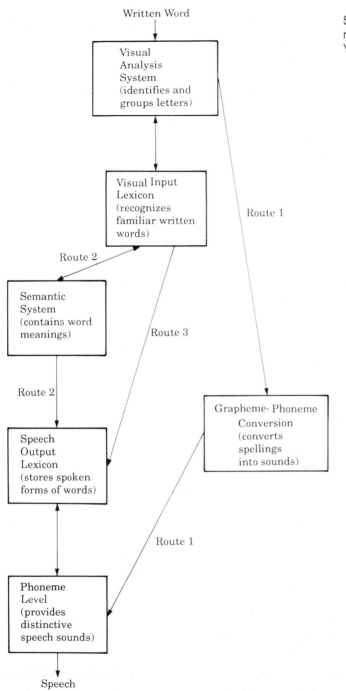

Written Word

Visual
Analysis
System
(identifies and
groups letters)

Visual Input
Lexicon
(recognizes
familiar written
words)

Route 1

Route 2

Semantic
System
(contains word
meanings)

Route 3

Route 2

Grapheme- Phoneme
Conversion
(converts
spellings
into sounds)

Speech
Output
Lexicon
(stores spoken
forms of words)

Route 1

Phoneme
Level
(provides
distinctive
speech sounds)

Speech

Some of the processes involved in
reading. Adapted from Ellis and
Young (1988).

reading words (see Ellis & Young, 1988, for a full discussion). The basic strategy adopted by cognitive neuropsychologists is to find patients who appear to be relying primarily on only one of the three routes between print and sound. Patients who are heavily reliant on Route 1 should be good at pronouncing regular words and non-words, but severely deficient at pronouncing irregular words.

Bub, Cancelliere, and Kertesz (1985) reported the case of a patient, MP, who could read approximately 90% of regular rare words correctly compared with only 40% of irregular rare words. Patients who rely primarily on either Route 2 or Route 3 should be reasonably good at saying familiar words whether regular or irregular, because specific information about their pronunciation is accessed. However, since they make little or no use of phoneme-grapheme conversion rules, they should perform poorly with unfamiliar words and non-words. The main difference between those using Route 2 and those using Route 3 is that the former should understand the meaning of the words and the latter should not. Beauvois and Derousne (1979) reported the case of a patient, RG, who appeared to be using Route 2. RG correctly read (and understood) 100% of real words, but was able to pronounce only 10% of non-words. So far as Route 3 is concerned, there is the case of WLP, a 62-year-old woman suffering from senile dementia. She was quite good at reading familiar regular and irregular words, but the words seemed to have practically no meaning for her.

Speech perception

We mentioned earlier in this chapter that only approximately 50% of words taken from spoken sentences and then presented on their own could be identified correctly (Lieberman, 1963). As we can usually make out what people are saying to us, this suggests that we make extensive use of contextual information when listening to speech. In slightly more technical terms, it seems reasonable to assume that speech perception involves top-down or conceptually driven processes based on the listener's expectations formed from contextual information as well as bottom-up or data-driven processes triggered by the spoken words themselves (see Chapter 1 for a discussion of the distinction between bottom-up and top-down processes).

Strong evidence that top-down processes can be involved in speech perception was obtained by Warren and Warren (1970), who studied what is known as the *phonemic restoration effect*. They presented their subjects with one of the following spoken sentences, with the asterisk indicating that a part of the sentence had been deleted:

1. It was found that the *eel was on the axle.
2. It was found that the *eel was on the shoe.
3. It was found that the *eel was on the table.
4. It was found that the *eel was on the orange.

In spite of the fact that all of the subjects heard the same speech sound "eel", its interpretation was markedly affected by the sentence context. Those subjects who listened to the first sentence reported hearing "wheel", whereas those listening to sentences two, three, and four heard "heel", "meal", and "peel" respectively. In other words, perception of "eel" was largely determined by top-down or conceptually driven processes.

The cohort model of speech perception

William Marslen-Wilson and Lorraine Tyler (1980) proposed an interactive model in which they attempted to spell out the ways in which bottom-up and top-down processes interact in speech perception. Some of the key features of their cohort model of speech perception are as follows:

- At a relatively early stage in the auditory presentation of a word, all of those words which are consistent with the sound sequence that has been heard so far become active; this set of words is known as the "word-initial cohort".
- Words belonging to the word-initial cohort are gradually eliminated either because they are inconsistent with subsequent sounds or because they do not fit the sentence context.
- Processing of the spoken word only has to continue until a point has been reached at which only one of the words in the word-initial cohort is consistent with the available evidence.

Marslen-Wilson and Tyler (1980) examined these theoretical notions in an experiment where the subjects task was to identify target words that were presented in spoken sentences. The target word was a member of a given category, a word that rhymed with a given word, or a word that was identical to a given word. The target word had to be identified as rapidly as possible. The sentences were normal sentences, syntactic sentences (grammatically correct but meaningless), or random sentences consisting of a sequence of unrelated words. What would be predicted from the theory proposed by Marslen-Wilson and Tyler (1980)? Since contextual information is used to restrict the number of possibilities that are considered, it follows that the target should be detected quickest when the sentence context provides useful information about grammar and meaning (i.e. the normal sentences) and slowest when the sentence context

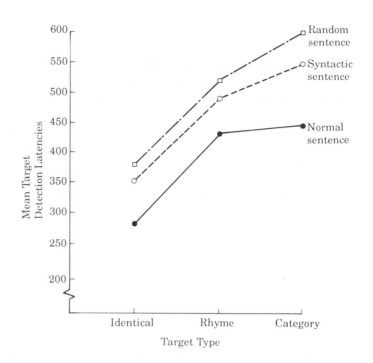

Detection latencies for word targets presented in sentences. Adapted from Marslen-Wilson and Tyler, 1980.

is uninformative (i.e. the random sentences). As can be seen in the figure above, this is exactly what happened.

The theoretical approach advocated by Marslen-Wilson and Tyler (1980) receives additional support if we consider in more detail the speed of response to the target words in the normal sentence condition. When the target word was identical to the given word, subjects responded approximately 200 milliseconds after the onset of the word. This is remarkably fast in view of the fact that the mean spoken duration of the target words used was 369 milliseconds. There would normally be several words which would be consistent with the part of the word presented in the first 200 milliseconds, which indicates that contextual information is used very early on in processing.

While the findings of Marslen-Wilson and Tyler (1980) are of interest, it is not entirely clear whether similar findings would be obtained under different circumstances. They used rather artificial tasks which may have led subjects to process speech in unusual ways. In addition, they presented their sentences in good listening conditions. When Bard, Shillcock, and Altmann (1988) presented sentences under less favourable conditions, they discovered that their subjects utilised the subsequent context, rather than the preceding context, to identify the words in each sentence.

Lip-reading

It has been known for a very long time that those who are hard of hearing make use of the visual information conveyed by the movements of the lips in speaking in order to facilitate the task of understanding what is being said to them. However, since the information conveyed by speech sounds tends to be less clear than that conveyed by written text, it could be argued that even those with perfectly normal hearing might benefit from lip-reading. The classic study to investigate lip-reading in those with normal hearing was carried out by McGurk and MacDonald (1976). They used a videotape of someone repeating "ba" several times. However, they altered the sound channel so that what was presented auditorily was someone saying "ga" over and over again in synchronisation with the lip movements. What the subjects reported was that they heard the sound "da", and not "ga" or "ba". In other words, the visual information was crucial in determining what was heard, and there was an almost literal blending of the visual and auditory information in perception.

Language comprehension

Most of the research and theories discussed in this section of the chapter are concerned with the comprehension of text, but the assumption is that they are also relevant to speech comprehension. If we assume that the processes involved in text comprehension are by and large the same processes as those involved in speech comprehension, then it should follow that those who have good reading skills should also tend to have good speech comprehension skills, whereas those who are poor at reading should also tend to be poor at understanding speech. This does, in fact, seem to be the case (Daneman & Carpenter, 1980).

Reading and speech comprehension both involve several processes. In addition to the basic processes already discussed, it is important for the reader or listener to take account of the grammatical structure and the meaning of what is being presented. It is a knowledge of grammar which allows us to realise that the following similar looking sentences convey a very different message: "The man bit the dog" and "The dog bit the man".

Meaning is extracted from text or speech by relating what is presented to information stored in long-term memory. There have been several attempts to explain how our previous knowledge is applied to text and speech, and some of these attempts will be discussed shortly.

While some theorists (e.g. Chomsky) have assumed that grammatical or syntactic processing occurs before semantic processing, the interactive model of Marslen-Wilson and Tyler (1980) is based on the assumption that

"I'M SURE WOLFIE DIDN'T MEAN IT DEAR...I THINK HE'S LEARNT HIS LESSON..."

this is not necessarily the case. Relevant evidence was obtained by Peter Herriot (1969). He discovered that it took longer to decide on the identity of the actor and the acted-upon in passive sentences (e.g. "Brenda was loved by Keith") than in active sentences (e.g. "Keith loved Brenda"). This could be explained by arguing that passive sentences are more complex syntactically than active sentences, and that syntactic processing occurs before processing of meaning. This explanation is not adequate, however, because it fails to account for some of Herriot's (1969) other findings. Consider sentences such as, "The lifeguard rescued the bather", and, "The bather was rescued by the lifeguard". Here it is reasonably clear from the meanings of the words who is likely to be actor and who the acted-upon. In these conditions, there was no difference in the time taken to respond to active and passive sentences. Thus, as the interactive model predicts, information about meaning can be used before syntactic processing is complete.

Grammar

One of the basic processes in comprehension is parsing, which involves working out the grammatical structure of a sentence. A straightforward demonstration of the importance of dividing a sentence up into its basic phrases or units was provided by Graf and Torrey (1966). They presented sentences visually line by line in such a way that each line consisted of a single unit or of parts of two different units. Here are examples of what they presented:

1.	2.
During World War II,	During World War
even fantastic schemes	II, even fantastic
received consideration	schemes received
if they gave promise	consideration if they gave
of shortening the conflict.	promise of shortening the
	conflict.

Not surprisingly, people found it much easier to understand the sentences when they were neatly divided into their appropriate units, as in the first example.

One of the main issues relating to parsing is whether it occurs rapidly as we listen to or read a sentence, or whether it is delayed until the end of the clause or the sentence. Most of the evidence suggests that parsing occurs as we listen to or read a sentence. One experimental approach involves using what is known as garden-path sentences, which are constructed so that the first attempt at parsing is likely to be in error. Kramer and Stevens (reported in Rumelhart, 1977) used several garden-path sentences, including the following: "The old man the boats"; "The steel ships are transporting is expensive." They found that subjects who were asked to read these sentences aloud tended to pause at that point in the sentence at which the initial parsing no longer made sense (between "man" and "boats" in the first sentence, and between "transporting" and "is expensive" in the second one).

There are certain characteristic features of the English language which can make the task of parsing a sentence into its constituent parts easier. For example, the words "because" and "which" are generally to be found at the beginning of a clause, whereas the words "a" and "the" usually occur at the start of a noun phrase. There is reasonable evidence that readers and listeners do take account of such features of the language when engaged in parsing (see Pullman, 1987).

In spite of the importance of parsing to an understanding of text and speech, it is generally the case that the grammatical features of sentences are not well remembered. This was shown strikingly by Johnson-Laird and Stevenson (1970). Their subjects were presented with short stories including sentences such as "John liked the painting and bought it from the duchess". When their memory for individual sentences was tested shortly afterwards, many subjects mistakenly claimed that they had been presented with the following sentence: "The painting pleased John and the duchess sold it to him." In other words, the meaning of the original sentence had been retained, but not the grammatical form in which that meaning had been expressed.

In spite of the impressive findings of Johnson-Laird and Stevenson (1970), it would not be accurate to assume that we always remember the gist of what we read or hear rather than the exact wording. As Keenan, MacWhinney, and Mayhew (1977) pointed out, the sentences used in laboratory studies generally have no personal significance for the subjects. Keenan et al. (1977) made a tape recording of students participating in a discussion. Subsequently, they tested the students' ability to recognise sentences which had been directed at them. The key finding was that there was good memory for the exact wording of sentences which possessed personal relevance (e.g. "Why are you so slow-witted?").

Context effects

When we are trying to understand a sentence, we often make use of information that is not contained directly within the sentence itself. This is known as contextual information, and we can usefully follow Margaret Harris and Max Coltheart (1986) in distinguishing between two kinds of context: general and specific. *General context effects* occur when our general knowledge about the world influences language comprehension. *Specific context effects* involve information obtained from earlier parts of a discourse.

General context effects occur all the time, because a crucial aspect of language comprehension involves making use of any relevant general knowledge that we possess. This can be demonstrated at an anecdotal level. When the author first visited the United States, he was baffled by the commentaries on baseball games. He could understand each word and sentence at some level, but full comprehension was impossible because of his imperfect knowledge of the rules of baseball.

Specific context effects can operate in a similar fashion, as was shown by John Bransford and Marcia Johnson (1972). They gave their subjects the passage in the panel below:

The procedure is actually quite simple. First you arrange items into different groups. Of course one pile may be sufficient depending on how much there is to do. If you have to go somewhere else due to lack of facilities, that is the next step; otherwise, you are pretty well set. It is important not to overdo things. That is, it is better to do too few things at once rather than too many. In the short run this may not seem important but complications can easily arise. A mistake can be expensive as well. At first, the whole procedure will seem complicated. Soon, however, it will become just another facet of life. It is difficult to foresee any end to the necessity for this task in the immediate future, but then, one never can tell. After the procedure is completed one arranges the materials into their appropriate places. Eventually, they will be used once more and the whole cycle will then have to be repeated. However, that is part of life. [p. 722]

Subjects who were given this passage on its own found it (as you probably did) difficult to comprehend. Those who were provided with an appropriate context in the form of the title, "Washing clothes", on the other hand, found the same passage reasonably easy to understand.

Schemata and inference drawing

We saw in Chapter 4 that schemata, meaning packets of stored knowledge, play an important role in language processing. The study by Bransford and Johnson (1972), which we have just discussed, illustrates the point. Their passage could only be easily comprehended when subjects were provided with a title which allowed them to access their schematic knowledge about washing clothes.

Rumelhart and Norman (1983) identified the following features of schemata:

- Schemata can vary considerably in the information they contain, from the very simple to the very complex.
- Schemata are frequently organised hierarchically; for example, in addition to a rather general restaurant schema or script, we probably also have more specific restaurant schemata for different kinds of restaurant (e.g. fast-food places, up-market French restaurants, and so on).
- Schemata operate in a top-down or conceptually driven way to facilitate interpretation of environmental stimuli.

There are various characteristics of language processing which indicate the key role played by schematic and other stored knowledge. For example, language comprehension frequently requires us to go far beyond the literal meanings of the sentences we read or hear. Essential information is often only implied, so that it is necessary to draw inferences in order to understand fully what is intended. You might think that only rarely do inferences need to be drawn to fill in the gaps in discourse. Consider the following sentence: "Three turtles rested on a floating log, and a fish swam beneath them." Most of us would use our stored knowledge of spatial relationships to draw the inference that the fish swam beneath the log as well as beneath the three turtles. This sort of inference is drawn so effortlessly that we are generally unaware that we have drawn an inference at all.

How do we know that someone has drawn a particular inference? According to Bransford, Barclay, and Franks (1972), the inferences which people draw are stored in long-term memory along with information about the sentences actually presented. As a result, they will sometimes mistakenly believe on a subsequent memory test that they previously heard or saw an inference. Bransford et al. (1972) presented their subjects with sentences such as the one above about the fish and the turtles. Later on, they were given a test of recognition memory. Subjects were confident that they had previously been presented with sentences which they had actually heard before (i.e. "Three turtles rested on a floating log, and a fish swam beneath them"). They were equally confident, however, that they had heard sentences which involved an inference from what they had heard (e.g. "Three turtles rested on a floating log, and a fish swam beneath *it*" although in the actual sentence, the fish swam beneath *them*). This indicates that spontaneous spatial inferences are made.

No complete theory of what is involved in inference drawing is available. However, schemata or scripts presumably play a part. In our discussion of schemata in Chapter 4, we found that some of the errors observed in memory seem to reflect the use of schemata. For example, people made use of a restaurant schema or script to understand a story about Jack eating out at a restaurant. Subsequently, they falsely recognised sentences fitting into the schema but not actually included in the story (e.g. "Jack sat down at the table.") Schemata thus lead people to draw schema-relevant inferences which facilitate comprehension but which may impair memory.

An important theoretical issue is whether schematic knowledge is always used at the time of comprehension and storage or whether it is sometimes used at the time of retrieval. So far as inferences are concerned, there is reasonably strong evidence that many of them are drawn during the comprehension process. For example, Rayner and Pollatsek (1987) discussed a study in which the length of time that the eyes fixated on the various words in a text was measured. The fixation time on a word (e.g. "knife") was less if the same word had been presented before than if a general word had been used earlier in the text (e.g. "knife" rather than "weapon"). Presumably this happened because it took the subjects some time to work out that a knife was the weapon referred to previously. This long fixation of "knife" following "weapon" did not occur, however, if the reference to "weapon" had included sufficient information for the reader to make the inference that the weapon was indeed a knife. The implication is that the inference was drawn during comprehension of the word "weapon".

There is also evidence that retrieval processes can be systematically affected by prior knowledge in the form of schemata. Anderson and Pichert (1978) asked subjects to read a story about a house from the perspective of a prospective buyer or of a prospective burglar. After the subjects had recalled the story, they were then asked to recall the story

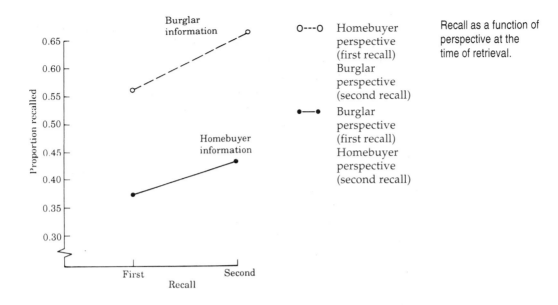

Recall as a function of perspective at the time of retrieval.

again on the basis of the alternative perspective. The key finding was that subjects recalled more information relevant to the alternative perspective on the second recall than on the first, presumably because the relevant schemata guided the recall process (see the figure above). As one of the subjects reported: "When he gave me the homebuyer perspective, I remembered the end of the story, you know, about the leak in the roof. The first time through I knew there was an ending, but I couldn't remember what it was. But it just popped into my mind when I thought about the story from the homebuyer perspective" (Anderson and Pichert, 1978, p. 10).

Story structure

Our comprehension of and memory for stories is highly *selective*, in the sense that we focus on the central theme of the story rather than on the relatively unimportant details. This was demonstrated convincingly by Gomulicki (1956). He asked one group of subjects to write a summary of a story that was visible in front of them. He asked a second group to read the story and then to recall it from memory. The third group of subjects were shown the summaries and the recalls, and were generally unable to tell which were which. These findings indicate that what is extracted from a story and then remembered closely resembles a summary in its emphasis on the main theme of that story.

Van Dijk and Kintsch (1983) have proposed a theory of story processing. They argued that a story is first of all processed so that the individual propositions (i.e. assertions that may be true or false) are extracted.

Evidence that propositions play a major role in sentence comprehension was obtained by Kintsch and Keenan (1973). They presented sentences which contained approximately the same number of words, but which varied in terms of the number of propositions. For example, the sentence, "Cleopatra's downfall lay in her foolish trust of the fickle political figures of the Roman world", contains twice as many propositions as the sentence, "Romulus, the legendary founder of Rome, took the women of the Sabine by force". Kintsch and Keenan (1973) discovered that reading time for such sentences increased by approximately one second for each additional proposition.

According to van Dijk and Kintsch (1983), the propositions of a story enter into a short-term working buffer of limited capacity, which is similar to the working memory system discussed in Chapter 4. When the buffer contains a number of propositions, the reader or listener tries to relate them to each other in a coherent fashion. In general terms, subsequent ability to remember the propositions depends on the length of time they spend in the working buffer. Those propositions which are highly relevant to the main theme of a story tend to be stored for a relatively long time in the working buffer. The reason is that such propositions are generally well connected to other propositions in the buffer, and so retaining them in the buffer facilitates the task of making coherent sense of the story. It follows from these theoretical assumptions that thematic information should be better remembered than non-thematic information, and we have already seen that this is the case (e.g. Gomulicki, 1956).

Van Dijk and Kintsch (1983) argued that there were additional processes involved in the task of understanding the gist or *macrostructure* of a story. More specifically, they claimed that readers or listeners make extensive use of their general knowledge to work out the major theme of a story. This leads to the production of *macropropositions*, which are general propositions used to form an overall macrostructure of the story.

There are substantial differences in the kinds of knowledge that individual people can bring to bear on story understanding. As a result, the way in which the working buffer is used and the story macrostructure which is formed will also differ from one person to the next. The theory proposed by van Dijk and Kintsch (1983), even though it has enhanced our understanding of story processing, suffers from the limitation that it is not precisely enough formulated to account in detail for such individual differences.

Language production

More is known about language comprehension than about language production. This is perhaps because it is generally easier for an experimenter to exercise control over the comprehension material than to constrain a subject's language production. Furthermore, language production cannot be considered purely from the perspective of a theory of language. Language production is very definitely a goal-directed activity, in the sense that people speak and write in order to make friends, influence people, convey information, and so on.

The two forms of language production considered in this chapter are speech production and writing. Speech production has been investigated more thoroughly than writing, but the reasons for this are not clear. The fact that most people spend far more of their time talking than writing may be a contributory factor, making an understanding of the processes involved in talking of more practical value.

Speech production

The usual approach in cognitive psychology is to set the subject a task, and then to assess how accurately or efficiently that task has been performed. This approach doesn't work, however, when we are investigating speech production. If we tell our subjects what we want them to say, then the spontaneity of normal speech is completely lost. If, on the other hand, we leave our subjects free to say whatever they like on a given topic, then we have very little experimental control over what is said. One approach is to ask people to speak on a particular topic, and to make a tape recording of what they say. Another, more useful approach is to ask people to make a collection of the speech errors which they make in everyday speech. As Gary Dell (1986) pointed out, "The inner workings of a highly complex system are often revealed by the way in which the system breaks down" (p. 284).

At a theoretical level, a promising start has been made by Garrett (1976; 1984). He argued that producing speech is a much more complex matter than it might appear to be from our everyday experience. According to his model, there are altogether five different levels of representation involved in speaking a sentence, and they occur in the following sequence:

- The *message-level representation*: this is an abstract, pre-linguistic representation of the idea or ideas that the speaker wants to communicate.
- The *functional-level representation*: this is an outline of the proposed utterance having grammatical structure; in other words, the slots for nouns, adjectives, and so on are allocated, but there are no actual words to fill the slots.
- The *positional-level representation*: this differs from the functional-level representation in that it incorporates the words of the sentence

that is to be produced.

- The *phonetic-level representation*: this indicates some of the necessary information about the ways in which words in the intended sentence are pronounced.
- The *articulatory-level representation*: this is the final representation, and contains a set of instructions for articulating the words in the sentence in the correct order.

This complex theory of speech production has not as yet been tested thoroughly. However, there is support for some of its major assumptions. In essence, Garrett (1984) claimed that the speaker engages in reasonably elaborate planning before beginning to speak. One way of testing this notion is to consider the sorts of error that people make while talking. If, for example, sounds or words from the end of a sentence intrude into the early part of a sentence, then this provides evidence for the notion of forward planning. The classic error of this type is the *spoonerism*, where the initial letter or letters of two words are transposed, named in honour of the Revd W. A. Spooner. Among the Revd Spooner's famous utterances was, "The Lord is a shoving leopard to his flock." Cynics have claimed that Spooner spent many hours thinking up spoonerisms, but there is no doubt that people do produce spoonerisms spontaneously.

Other errors also demonstrate the existence of forward planning. An *anticipation error* occurs when a word is spoken earlier in the sentence than it should be (e.g. "The school is at school.") A similar type of error is the *exchange error*, in which two items within a sentence are swapped (e.g. "This is the happiest life of my day.")

Pre-planning of speech is also shown by the high incidence of pausing shown by most speakers. It has been found that most people pause for approximately 40% or 50% of their total speaking time. These pauses occur mainly between one clause and the next, and seem to reflect the time taken to decide what to say next and how to say it. While pausing is very common in speech production, it may be wondered whether it is really *essential* to normal speech as Garrett's (1984) theory seems to imply. This issue was investigated by encouraging people telling stories to reduce the number of their long pauses. The encouragement was effective, but the repetition of words and even of whole phrases doubled. It thus appears that unfilled pauses are of crucial importance in the planning of spontaneous speech.

Further evidence that pauses are used for planning the next utterance comes from an analysis of the speaker's gaze patterns. Because looking at one's listener involves monitoring his or her behaviour and so uses some processing capacity, we might expect that the speaker would look less at the listener during the complex planning typically occurring during pausing. This prediction has been supported. In one study, speakers looked at their listeners 50% of the time between pauses, but only 20% of the time during pauses. If speakers did continue to look at their listeners during a pause, their speech tended to manifest an increased number of false starts and repetitions.

In general terms, the demands of speech production are so great that production of speech and planning for the next utterance are difficult to combine satisfactorily. Pauses are used in an attempt to ease these processing demands, but even with pauses, spontaneous speech is usually characterised by a variety of errors. The position is rather different when people have prepared the content (but not the wording) of what they intend to say (e.g. before a public lecture). Such prepared speech exhibits many fewer grammatical and stylistic errors than does spontaneous speech.

According to Garrett (1976; 1984), speakers decide on the grammatical structure of a proposed utterance in the functional-level representation, and then select the appropriate words to fit into that structure in the subsequent position-level representation. Given this sequence, it would be possible for the grammatical structure of a spoken sentence to be correct even though some of the words were incorrectly positioned. Precisely this is found with *morpheme-exchange errors*, in which the roots or basic forms of two words are switched leaving the grammatical structure unchanged (e.g. "He has already trunked two packs".)

Why is human speech production so prone to error? According to Dell (1986), it is the price we pay for having such a flexible speech-production system. Its flexibility has the great advantage of allowing us to produce novel sentences. Indeed, most speech errors involve novelty, but simply novelty of an unwanted kind. If we had a very rigid speech-production system, it might prevent errors from occurring, but we would suffer the disadvantage of very stereotyped utterances.

Written language

Written language differs from spoken language in a number of ways. The hesitations, grammatical errors, and interchanges of words characteristic of spoken language are largely, or entirely, absent from written language. It should therefore come as no surprise to discover that theories of the processes involved in writing differ significantly from those put forward to explain speech production.

One of the most detailed theories of the writing process was proposed by Hayes and Flower (1986). According to them, writing essentially consists of three inter-related processes:

- The *planning process*, which involves producing ideas and arranging them into a writing plan appropriate to the writer's goals.
- The *sentence generation process*, which translates the writing plan into actual sentences that can be written down.
- The *revision process*, which involves an evaluation of what has been written so far; this evaluation can encompass individual words at one extreme or the overall structure of the writing at the other extreme.

In general, the processes operate in the order planning, sentence generation, and revision; however it is quite common for the writer to return to the planning process after several sentences have been generated and revised, especially with longer pieces of writing.

Writing plans are obviously much influenced by the relevant knowledge that the writer possesses about the topic to be written about. Another less obvious factor determining the quality of the writing plan is *strategic knowledge*, which is knowledge of the methods used in constructing a writing plan in order to make it coherent and well-organised. Children often lack such strategic knowledge—they tend to make use of a *knowledge-telling strategy*, where they simply write down everything they can think of that is relevant to a topic without organising the information in any way (Scardamalia and Bereiter, 1987). Skilled writers, in contrast, possess strategic knowledge, which enables them to make use of a *knowledge-transforming strategy*. This involves focusing on potential problems within the planning process (e.g. "Are the main points arranged in the most logical order?").

The writing plan constructed during the planning process is generally much shorter and sketchier than the written story or essay itself. Kaufer, Hayes, and Flower (1986) asked writers to write down an outline of their essays corresponding to the writing plan. They discovered that the subsequent essay was always at least eight times longer than the outline. In order to understand more fully the processes involved in sentence generation, Kaufer et al. (1986) asked writers to think aloud while they were writing. Below is one such verbal protocol, with fragments 12 and 13 making up the sentence that was written down, and fragments 1, 4, 7, 9, and 11 representing the initial attempts to construct part of the sentence. The dashes indicate a pause of two seconds or more:

The best thing about it is (1)___what? (2) Something about using my mind (3) ___it allows me the opportunity to (4)___uh___I want to write something about my ideas (5)___to put ideas into action (6)___or___to develop my ideas into (7) ___what? (8)___into a meaningful form? (9) Oh,

Bleh!___say it allows me (10) ___to use (11)___Na___allows me___scratch
that. The best thing about it is that it allows me to use (12)___my mind and
ideas in a productive way (13).

Kaufer et al. (1986) discovered that expert writers produced larger
sentence fragments than less skilled writers: 11.2 words versus 7.3 words
on average. However, the similarities outweighed the differences. Both
groups of writers wrote down approximately 75% of the sentence fragments they produced in their verbal protocols. They also found that when
sentence parts were altered, it was almost always the last part to be
produced that was altered. One of the interesting and perhaps surprising
findings about the revision process is that expert writers typically spend
longer than non-expert writers on revision. There are two main reasons
for this. First, expert writers are more skilled at detecting errors that
require revision. For example, in a study by Hayes, Flower, Schriver,
Stratman, and Carey (1985), expert writers detected approximately 60%
more problems in a written text than did non-expert writers. Second,
expert writers tend to focus on the overall coherence and structure of what
has been written, whereas non-expert writers concentrate more on individual words and phrases. It takes much more time to change the structure
of a piece of writing than simply to alter some of the words.

How adequate is the theoretical approach to writing advocated by
Hayes and Flower (1986)? On the positive side, they have been reasonably
successful in identifying some of the major differences between strategies
used by expert and non-expert writers. This is of value in terms of
suggesting ways in which poor writers could improve their writing skills.

Probably the major limitation of their approach is the emphasis they
place on verbal protocols—i.e. the spoken thoughts of writers engaged in
writing. While there may be conscious awareness of many of the processes
involved in sentence generation and revision, it seems probable that much
of the planning process occurs below the conscious level and thus cannot
be verbalised.

Speech versus writing

You may have noticed that theoretical accounts of speech production
share some similarities with theories of the writing process. In particular,
both forms of language production involve deciding what message is to
be communicated and how it is to be expressed. Of course, there are also
some major differences. Apart from those discussed above, there is the
fact that people normally speak about six times faster than they write.

Gould (1978; 1980) has made a serious attempt to compare spoken and
written language, especially dictated versus written letters. In spite of the

normal sixfold speed advantage of spoken over written language, he discovered that even those with good dictation skills rarely dictate letters more than 35% faster than they can write them. Gould then videotaped his subjects while they were composing letters. The proportion of the time spent in different processes was approximately the same for dictated and written letters. For example, for both dictated and written letters, two-thirds of the total composition time was devoted to planning. Another way of comparing different modes of language production is to look at individual differences. If the skills involved are similar in each case, then those who are good at speaking or dictating should also tend to be good at writing. That is exactly what Gould (1979; 1980) found when he investigated the quality of letter composition. The implication is that the planning processes that decide on the message to be communicated are of central importance in language production. In comparison, the specific form of the communication (e.g. speech, writing) is of less psychological significance.

In spite of Gould's (1979; 1980) findings, there is other evidence which suggests that speaking and writing may differ in quite important ways. Cognitive neuropsychologists, who investigate cognitive functioning in brain-damaged patients, have addressed the issue of the similarity between speaking and writing. They have studied patients whose speech and/or writing is severely impaired. If speaking and writing depend on the same processes and structures, then the expectation is that both or neither will be impaired in any given patient. This is generally the case, but there are interesting exceptions.

Take the example of an engineer, EB, who suffered a stroke that prevented him from using either inner speech (i.e. talking silently to himself) or overt speech. In spite of his virtually non-existent ability to produce speech, EB's written language was reasonably good, as we can see from this description of his first memories after his stroke:

> Gradually after what seemed days and days, got back enough strength to pull myself up and sit if I held on. I tilted off to the right and had a hard time maintaining my balance. The nurse and doctor and an orderly helped me up then ... I got to another part of the hospital where there were two doctors asking me questions I couldn't answer. (Levine, Calvanio, & Popovics, 1982).

Cognitive neuropsychologists have also discovered cases where patients can speak fluently but are scarcely able to write at all. Then there are other patients who make very different errors in speaking and in writing, supporting the view that there are major differences in the processes underlying these two forms of language production. More specifically, the evidence accumulated by cognitive neuropsychologists indicates that information about the spoken and the written forms of words is stored separately. This means that brain damage sometimes selectively disrupts only writing or only speaking.

Speaking and writing thus resemble each other in that they both depend on the same knowledge base and on rather similar planning processes which determine the structure of language production. However, dissimilarities between speaking and writing become greater as processing progresses towards the spoken or written word, and it is these later processes that have been studied by cognitive neuropsychologists.

Language and thought

One of the most important and puzzling issues in cognitive psychology concerns the relationship between language and thought. At least in adults, language and thought seem to be reasonably closely related, but theorists have disagreed as to whether language determines thought, or whether it is more a question of thought determining language.

One of the earliest attempts by psychologists to provide a theoretical account of the relationship between language and thought was made by the Behaviourists. They were reluctant to speculate on the many complex internal processes involved in thinking; instead, the originator of Behaviourism (John B. Watson) argued in an incautious moment that thinking was nothing more than sub-vocal speech. It may be true that most people sometimes engage in inner speech when thinking about difficult problems, but that is a far cry from Watson's dogmatic theoretical position.

The ludicrous nature of Watson's theory was revealed in a witty comment by the philosopher Herbert Feigel. According to Feigel, Watson "made up his windpipe that he had no mind." Experimental evidence destroying Watson's theory was provided by Smith, Brown, Toman, and Goodman (1947). Dr Smith showed great bravery by allowing himself to be given a curare derivative (curare was the poison used by American Indians on their arrow-heads). This paralysed his entire musculature, so that an artificial respirator had to be used to keep him alive. Since the curare totally prevented any sub-vocal speech, it should also have prevented him from thinking. In fact, after he had recovered from his ordeal, he reported that he had been able to think about what was going on around him while paralysed.

John Watson (1878–1958). An American psychologist who became world famous as the founder of behaviourism during the 1910s. He started his career as a student of animal learning, but gradually developed a major interest in the larger issue of how psychology could become a science. His proposed answer that psychologists should concentrate only on what can be directly observed had an enormous impact on psychological research. His academic career came to an abrupt halt in 1920 because of a divorce scandal. However, he bounced back by applying conditioning principles to advertising, becoming an influential figure in the advertising world.

Whorf's theory of linguistic relativity

One of the most influential theorists on the relationship between thought and language is Benjamin Lee Whorf (1956). He was a fire prevention officer for an insurance company who spent his spare time working in linguistics. Whorf was much influenced by the fact that there are obvious differences between the world's languages. For example, Eskimo has approximately one hundred words to refer to different snow and ice conditions, and Arabic has numerous words describing camels and their disgusting habits.

There are other differences which may be more important. In the Thai language, verbs do not have tenses as they do in English. As a result, a Thai girl who was staying with the family of the author spoke English quite well, but had great difficulty in using verbs correctly to refer to the past or to the future. Whorf was impressed by these differences between languages, and so proposed his hypothesis of *linguistic relativity*, according to which language determines, or has a major influence on, thinking. In his own words, the linguistic system is:

> ... not merely a reproducing instrument for viewing ideas but rather is itself the shaper of ideas, the program and guide for the individual's mental activity, for his analysis of impressions, for his synthesis of his original stock in trade. Formulation of ideas is not an independent process ... but is part of a particular grammar and differs, from slightly to greatly, as between different grammars. We dissect nature along lines laid down by our native language. [pp. 212–213].

It is not easy to test the Whorfian hypothesis directly. Some clarification of the theoretical issues involved was offered by Miller and McNeill (1969). They suggested that there are really three different hypotheses concerning the effects of language on psychological processes. The strong hypothesis (that espoused by Whorf) claims that language determines thinking. The weak hypothesis states that language affects perception. Finally, the weakest hypothesis makes the more modest claim that language influences memory in such a way that information which is easily described in a particular language will be remembered better than information which is difficult to describe in that language. Of these three hypotheses, the weakest hypothesis has been tested most often.

Apparent support for Whorf's position was obtained by Lenneberg and Roberts (1956), who discovered that Zuni speakers made more mistakes in recognising yellows and oranges than did English speakers. Since the

Zuni language differs from English in having only a single word to describe yellows and oranges, it could be argued that the impoverished Zuni language led to memorial problems.

Most subsequent research has produced findings less favourable to Whorf's hypothesis. Eleanor Heider (1972) used as her starting point the fact that English (and other languages) have the same basic eleven colour words, and for each colour there is a best or focal colour. The importance of these focal colours is shown by the finding that English speakers generally find it easier to remember focal colours than non-focal ones. If it is true that language affects memory, there would be no reason to expect the same results with the Dani, who are a Stone Age tribe living in New Guinea. The Dani language has only two basic colour words: "mili" to refer to dark, cold colours, and "mola" to describe bright, warm colours. In spite of the impoverishment of the Dani language, the Dani people showed better recognition memory for focal than for non-focal colours. This can probably be explained by the fact that focal colours are processed specially because of the basic physiology of colour vision. Other investigators have reported similar findings to those of Heider (1972), and it appears that language does not have any major influence on the ways in which colour is perceived and remembered.

Some evidence that language can have a modest effect on perception and/or memory was obtained by Carmichael, Hogan, and Walter (1932). Subjects were shown a series of stimulus figures, and were told that each one resembled some well-known object. As the figure below shows, subsequent reproductions of the figures from memory were influenced by the verbal descriptions that had been provided for each object.

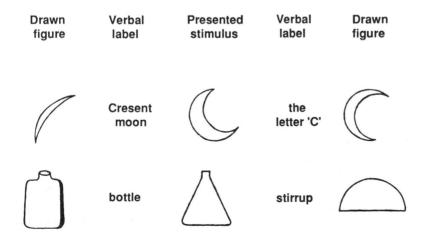

Drawn figure	Verbal label	Presented stimulus	Verbal label	Drawn figure
	Cresent moon		the letter 'C'	
	bottle		stirrup	

The work of Bernstein (1973) is of relevance to the notion that language influences at least some aspects of thought. He argued that a child's use of language is determined in part by the social environment in which it grows up. He distinguished between two language codes or patterns of speech which he termed the *restricted code* and the *elaborated code*. The restricted code is relatively concrete and descriptive; it is also generally context-dependent, in the sense that it is difficult to understand unless one knows the context in which it is used. In contrast, the elaborated code is more complex and abstract, and it can be understood without information about the context. Bernstein (1973; p. 203) gave the following examples of the two codes based on descriptions of four pictures showing (1) boys playing football, (2) the ball going through a house window, (3) a woman looking out of the window and a man making an angry gesture, and (4) the children retreating:

- Restricted code: "They're playing football and he kicks it and it goes through there it breaks the window and they're looking at it and he comes out and shouts at them because they've broken it so they run away and then she looks out and she tells them off."
- Elaborated code: "Three boys are playing football and one boy kicks the ball and it goes through the window the ball breaks the window and the boys are looking at it and a man comes out and shouts at them because they've broken the window so they run away and then that lady looks out of her window and she tells the boys off."

Bernstein (1973) argued that middle-class children generally use the elaborated code, whereas working-class children use the restricted code. However, he also pointed out that many middle-class children can use both codes, whereas many working-class children are limited to the restricted code. It seems possible that the lack of an elaborated code of language might limit the thinking of working-class children. However, Bernstein claimed that there are class differences in the use of language, but that these differences do not extend to basic language competence or understanding of language. As a consequence, users of the restricted code are not at a disadvantage. It has proved difficult to test these claims, and the available evidence is inconclusive.

We have seen that there is relatively little support for the view that thought is influenced by language. However, the opposite hypothesis (i.e. that language is influenced by thought) makes some sense. After all, young children begin to think some time before they acquire language, and so it is possible that language develops as an instrument for communicating thoughts. Eskimos may have many words to describe snow and

Arabs may have several terms to refer to camels because their life experiences require them to think in a very precise way about these aspects of their environment.

Jean Piaget was a prominent supporter of the view that thought influences language. According to him, children unable to solve a particular linguistic problem would still be unable to do so, even if they were taught the relevant linguistic skills possessed by most children who can solve the problem. This prediction was confirmed by Sinclair-de-Zwart (1969). Language did not appear to facilitate thought in this study, and the possession of the relevant linguistic skills was of use only when it had been preceded by mastery of the necessary cognitive skills.

An important alternative to the theories discussed so far was put forward by Lev Vygotsky (1934). According to him, language and thought have quite separate origins. Thinking develops because of the need to solve problems, whereas language arises because the child wants to communicate and to keep track of his or her internal thoughts. The child initially finds it difficult to distinguish between these two functions of language, but subsequently they become clearly separated as external and internal speech. External speech tends to be more coherent and complete than internal speech.

As the child develops, so language and thought become less independent of each other. Their inter-dependence can be seen in what Vygotsky referred to as "verbal thought". However, thought can occur without the intervention of language, as in using a tool. The opposite process (i.e. language being used without active thought processes being involved) can also happen; an example cited by Vygotsky is repeating a poem which has been thoroughly over-learned.

The task of investigating the relationship between language and thought is so complex that no definitive answers are available. However, it seems far more likely that language is the servant of thought rather than its master. It also seems likely that there is some validity in Vygotsky's claim that thought and language are partially independent of each other.

Summary: Language comprehension and production

- Linguistic communications are usually presented to us in the form of written text or speech. While the process of comprehension appears to be similar in both cases, some of the initial stages of processing differ.
- Analysis of eye movements during reading has revealed that all of the information from text is extracted during the perceptual span.
- The task of reading aloud reveals that there are a number of different routes between seeing the printed word and saying it.
- The fact that the speech signal is often somewhat ambiguous means that speech perception often relies heavily on top-down or conceptually driven processes. Speech perception is also facilitated by lip-reading.
- The comprehension process involves parsing—i.e. working out the grammatical structure of the sentence. The interpretation of a sentence is often influenced by context effects, either general knowledge or information from earlier parts of the communication. Schemata are especially useful in the task of drawing inferences and filling in gaps in the information provided by speech or by text. Comprehension focuses on the central theme or themes of what is presented.
- The psychological factors involved in speech production have been investigated by examining the kinds of error that people make while speaking. One of the most obvious features of speech is the emphasis on forward planning.
- Writing involves the three processes of planning, sentence generation, and revision. Expert writers differ from non-expert ones in a number of ways, especially in their focus on the overall structure and coherence of what they are writing.
- The relationship between language and thought has been considered by many theorists. It seems more likely that thought has some influence over language.

Further reading

Most of the topics discussed in this chapter are explored in more detail in M.W. Eysenck and M.T. Keane (1990), *Cognitive Psychology: A Student's Handbook* (Hove, U.K.: Lawrence Erlbaum Associates Ltd.). J. Greene (1986), *Language Understanding: A Cognitive Approach* (Milton Keynes: Open University Press) deals with most aspects of language comprehension in an approachable way.

Thinking 6

Several different definitions of thinking have been offered over the years. According to Charles Osgood (1953), thinking occurs whenever behaviour is produced for which "the relevant cues are not available in the external environment at the time the correct response is required, but must be supplied by the organism itself" (p. 656). While this definition seems to capture part of what is involved in thinking, it is too general. For example, simply recalling information from long-term memory would often fit Osgood's definition, but would seem to lack the complexity of processing usually associated with thinking.

A more adequate definition of thinking was offered by Humphrey (1951). He suggested that thinking is "what happens in experience when an organism, human or animal, meets, recognises and solves a problem" (p. 311). Humphrey's definition is reasonably satisfactory, but begs the question of what we mean by a "problem".

This issue was addressed by John Anderson (1980), who argued that the activity of problem solving typically involves the following three ingredients:

- The individual is goal-directed, in the sense of attempting to reach a desired end state.
- Reaching the goal or solution requires a sequence of mental processes rather than simply a single mental process; putting your foot on the brake when you see a red light is goal-directed behaviour, but the single process involved does not usually involve thinking.
- The mental processes involved in the task should be cognitive rather than automatic; this ingredient needs to be included to eliminate routine sequences of behaviour, such as dealing a pack of cards.

Even though thinking may always involve a problem of some kind, the topic of thinking is traditionally divided into a number of more specific topics, including problem solving, reasoning, and decision making and judgement. These traditional divisions are followed in this chapter. It should be noted, however, that many of the same cognitive processes span these different areas of study.

Problem solving

Problem solving has been investigated in a number of different ways over the years. Much of the early research addressed the issue of the problem-solving skills of animals rather than humans, and produced somewhat inconclusive results. This was followed by a considerable amount of research on the effects of past experience on problem solving. A recent approach involves comparing individuals at different levels of expertise in terms of the strategies they adopt during problem solving. The goal of such research is to identify those processes and strategies which lead to successful problem-solving performance.

The computational or cognitive science approach to problem solving, based on the notion that human problem solving can be simulated on a computer, is becoming increasingly important. These diverse approaches to problem solving are all considered in this section of the chapter.

Early research

The first systematic attempt to study thinking or problem solving was carried out by Thorndike (1898). A cat was placed in a puzzle box, from which it could escape only by making a rather arbitrary response, such as clawing at a loop of string. The cat seemed to behave in an unintelligent fashion, squeezing the bars, running around the box, jumping on things, and so on. Eventually the right response was made by accident, and over subsequent trials the animal gradually became faster at making its escape. According to Thorndike (1898), learning occurred by means of trial and error—that is, the animal responded randomly until one response happened to be successful.

A very different theoretical view of problem solving and thinking was proposed by the Gestaltists in the early years of this century. They claimed that solving a problem requires reorganising the various features of the problem situation in an appropriate way. This reorganisation typically involves a flash of insight or the "aha" experience. A number of examples of insight were provided by Wolfgang Kohler (1925), a Gestalt psychologist who spent much time during the First World War studying the thinking of apes on the island of Tenerife. In one experiment he arranged things so that none of the sticks in an ape's cage was long enough for the ape to use it to reach out and draw in a banana. The ape spent some time pondering what to do. After a period of thought, the ape apparently had a flash of insight. He leapt up and joined two sticks together, and used this elongated stick to obtain the banana.

Thorndike, with his cat in a box, regarded problem solving (at least in animals) as a very slow and laborious business, whereas the Gestaltists argued that problem solving could be very fast and efficient when the appropriate insight was experienced. Some of the differences between the two theories can be accounted for by the different sorts of task used. Thorndike's puzzle box did not really permit insight to occur, whereas in Kohler's task there was a meaningful relationship between the animal's responses and their impact on the problem. Nowadays most psychologists would argue that both theories are somewhat misguided. Thinking and problem solving are usually more purposive than Thorndike allowed for, and insight is a rarer commodity than the Gestaltists imagined.

From the perspective of cognitive psychology, what we want to know about thinking is what processes are involved. An early attempt to provide this knowledge was the theory put forward by Graham Wallas (1926). He suggested that thinking and problem solving involve a total of four stages:

- *Preparation*, in which relevant information is collected and initial solution attempts are made.
- *Incubation*, in which the individual stops thinking consciously about the problem.
- *Illumination*, in which the way to solve the problem appears suddenly in an insightful way.
- *Verification*, in which the solution is checked for accuracy.

The most suprising part of Wallas's theory is the idea that complex problem solving benefits from a period of incubation. However, there is some experimental evidence which supports the notion of incubation. Silveira (1971) gave her subjects the following problem.

The necklace problem. There are four separate pieces of chain, and each of them consists of three links; all of the links within each piece are closed; it costs two cents to open a link and three cents to close one; the 12 links of chain must be joined up to form a single circular chain necklace at a cost of no more than 15 cents.

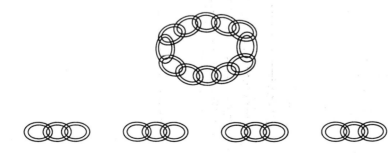

The necklace problem used by Silveira (1971).

Only 55% of those who worked solidly at this problem solved it within 30 minutes, whereas 64% of those who took a 30-minute break during the task did so, and the success rate rose to 85% among those who had a four-hour break. Presumably the incubation period served the function of reducing the tendency of subjects to fixate on inappropriate methods of attempting to solve the problem. The solution is as follows: Open all three links in one chain at a cost of six cents. Then use these three open links to join together the other three pieces of chain at a further cost of nine cents, making a total of 15 cents.

There is also anecdotal evidence from leading thinkers and scientists to support the notion of incubation. For example, here is a quotation from the outstanding French mathematician, Poincare (given in Ghiseli, 1952):

> The changes of travel made me forget my mathematical work. Having reached Coutances, we entered an omnibus to go some place or other. At the moment when I put my foot on the step the idea came to me, without anything in my former thoughts seeming to have paved the way for it, that the transformations I had used to define the Fuchsian functions were identical with those of non-Euclidian geometry. [p. 37]

Past experience

In general terms, our ability to think effectively and to solve problems rapidly increases as we accumulate experience. This beneficial effect of past experience is technically known as a *positive transfer effect*.

People do not always use relevant past experience in an appropriate fashion, however, as was demonstrated by Gick and Holyoak (1980). They considered a problem known as Duncker's radiation problem, in which a patient with a malignant tumour in his stomach could only be saved by a special kind of ray. The problem was that a ray of sufficient strength to destroy the tumour would also destroy the healthy tissue, whereas a ray that was not strong enough to harm healthy tissue would be too weak to destroy the tumour.

Only about 10% of the subjects were able to solve this problem. The answer is to direct several low-intensity rays at the tumour from different directions. Other subjects were given three stories to memorise, one of which was conceptually related to the radiation problem (it was about a general capturing a fortress by having his army converge at the same time on the fortress along several different roads). When the subjects were told that one of the three stories might be relevant to solving the radiation problem, 92% of the subjects solved it. When the hint was not offered, however, those given the stories to memorise did no better than those

The Duncker (1945) experiment. Subjects were told to mount a candle on a vertical screen, using these materials.

given no stories at all. In other words, the fact that relevant information is stored in long-term memory is no guarantee that it will be used.

There are various other situations in which previous learning can actually seriously disrupt thinking processes and problem solving. This *negative transfer effect* has been demonstrated many times under laboratory conditions. For example, Duncker (1945) used an experiment where the task was to mount a candle on a vertical screen. Various objects were spread around, including a box full of tacks and a book of matches (illustrated above).

The solution involved using the box as a platform for the candle, but subjects found it difficult to think of the correct answer. The subjects' past experience presumably led them to regard the box as a container rather than a platform. Further evidence for this interpretation came from the finding that subjects performed better when the box was initially empty rather than full of tacks—the latter set-up emphasised the container-like quality of the box.

Duncker's study (1945) involves a phenomenon known as *functional fixedness*. This is the tendency to think (on the basis of past experience) that objects can be used only for a very narrow range of functions. From a scientific point of view, the difficulty with such studies is that we really do not know in detail about the subjects" relevant past experience (e.g. with boxes). A preferable approach is to supply the subjects with the relevant past experience during the course of the experiment, and then to see what the effects are on later performance. This was done in a famous series of experiments by Luchins (1942). He used water-jar problems. These involved three water jars of varying capacity. The subject's task was to imagine pouring water from one jar to another in order to finish up with a specified amount of water in one of the jars.

The most striking finding obtained by Luchins can be illustrated by considering in a little detail one of his experiments. One of the problems was as follows: Jar A can hold 28 quarts of water, Jar B 76 quarts, and Jar C 3 quarts. The task is to end up with exactly 25 quarts in one of the jars. I am sure all the readers of this book can work out the answer: Jar A is filled, and then Jar C is filled from it, which conveniently leaves exactly 25 quarts in Jar A. Ninety-five per cent of subjects who had previously been given similar problems solved it. However, of those subjects who had been trained on a series of problems, all of which had complex three-jar solutions (unlike this simple two-jar solution), only 36% managed to solve this relatively simple problem. These findings led Luchins (1942) to the following conclusion: "Einstellung—habituation—creates a mechanised state of mind, a blind attitude towards problems; one does not look at the problem on its own merits but is led by a mechanical application of a used method" (p. 15).

Some clarification of why it is that past experience sometimes impairs our ability to solve a current problem was obtained by Levine (1971). The task he used involved the presentation of a series of cards, each bearing letters "A" and "B", with one letter on the left and the other letter on the right. For the first several problems, the experimenter explained to the subject that the solution involved a position sequence (e.g. the letter on the left should be selected on the first card, the letter on the right on the second card, and so on alternately). The subject then said "A" or "B" after each card was presented, and the experimenter indicated whether the response was correct. According to Levine (1971), these problems led the subjects to predict that the solution to subsequent problems would always involve a position sequence. In his terminology, the range of possible position sequences forms a *hypothesis set*, and the subject will work through all of the possible solutions in that hypothesis set before deciding to select a different hypothesis set.

Levine's (1971) theoretical views led to an interesting prediction. The number of possible position sequences is extremely large. It follows that subjects who are given several problems involving position sequences, and then a very simple problem not involving a position sequence, will probably fail to solve it. That is exactly what Levine (1971) found. After his subjects had become used to position sequence solutions, he used a problem in which the selection of the letter "A" was always correct and selection of the letter "B" was always incorrect. In spite of the apparently trivial nature of the problem, approximately 80% of university students failed to solve it within 100 trials. When these non-solvers were then asked to select the correct solution from a choice of six possibilities, none of them was successful!

It is usual for textbooks to focus on studies like those of Duncker, Luchins, and Levine in order to emphasise the inadequacies of thinking that can result from making inappropriate use of past experience. Our thinking is, of course, sometimes unduly constrained in this way. It is usually the case, however, that the best way to tackle a new problem is to try to make use of our previous experience with similar problems. The fact that adults can solve most problems far more rapidly than children provides striking evidence of the advantages of past experience. In other words, while past experience sometimes interferes with problem solving, it generally has a helpful effect.

Expertise: novices and experts

One way of attempting to understand more about the ways in which past experience can be beneficial to problem solving is to compare the performance of novices and experts. While we would all agree that experts possess much more relevant knowledge than novices, it is a matter of some controversy as to whether this is the most important reason for their superior performance. We can presume that experts have also developed more effective strategies and processes than novices, and it is the combination of greater knowledge and better strategies that accounts for their expertise.

Chess playing expertise. The first problem-solving situation in which the differences between experts and novices were investigated systematically was a game of chess. There are a number of reasons why chess is a good choice.

- First, the differences between experts and novices are relatively clear-cut, because experts will have devoted hundreds or thousands of hours to chess playing.
- Second, the complexity of chess means that the study of expert chess players is likely to be informative about high-level skills of thinking.
- Third, the fact that most games consist of dozens of moves means that we have a lot of information about the strategies followed by chess players during the course of a game.

Some of the intriguing findings that have emerged from the study of chess are considered in this section.

The search for the secret of chess playing expertise was initiated by De Groot (1966). In one of his studies, he asked grand masters and expert players to think aloud when selecting their moves. You might expect that grand masters would consider more alternative moves than expert players, or that they would think through the implications of making each of these moves in more detail. Surprisingly, the two groups did not differ in either respect, in spite of the fact that the grand masters made superior moves. It should be noted, however, that subsequent research (see Holding, 1989) has indicated that strong players do generally think further ahead than do weaker players.

De Groot (1966) was more successful in finding differences between chess players varying in expertise when he tested his assumption that grand masters have many more board positions stored in long-term memory. He presented board positions from actual games for five seconds, and then asked chess players to reconstruct these positions. Grand masters had a 91% success rate for reconstructing board positions, whereas less expert players were correct only 41% of the time. However, the two groups did not differ in their ability to reconstruct the board positions when the pieces were arranged randomly. The implication is that grand masters can relate actual board positions to their stored knowledge of previous games, and that this knowledge facilitated performance.

Further support for the notion that the number of stored positions is important was obtained by Simon and Gilmartin (1973). They developed two versions of a computer model called the Memory-Aided Pattern Perceiver (MAPP), with one version having access to more stored chess patterns than the other (1114 versus 894 patterns). The version with the greater number of patterns was better at reconstructing chess positions. A comparison between the performance of MAPP and that of chess masters at reconstructing chess positions suggested to Simon and Gilmartin (1973) that masters probably have somewhere between 10,000 and 100,000 chess patterns in long-term memory.

Clearly, learning all the words in the dictionary would not enable us to write like Shakespeare. Similarly, it seems improbable that a master level of chess playing involves no more than learning several thousand chess positions. Relevant evidence was obtained by Holding and Reynolds (1982). First of all, they confirmed the finding of De Groot (1966) that better players do not differ from inferior ones in their ability to reconstruct random board positions. This indicated that the better players had no relevant chess patterns stored in long-term memory. In spite of this, the more expert players were able to suggest better moves than the less expert ones when asked to decide on the best move to make from the same random board positions. These findings suggest that the expert players possessed superior strategic skills as well as simply more knowledge of chess positions.

The computational approach

There has been increasing interest over the years in the notion that it may be possible to program computers to mimic the problem-solving behaviour of people. Allen Newell and Herb Simon (e.g., 1972) were the first researchers to produce systematic computer simulations of human problem solving with their General Problem Solver, and they have probably been more influential than anyone else in the area of problem solving. They started their research by asking people to solve problems, and to think aloud while they were working on the problems. They then used these verbal reports as the basis for deciding what general strategy tended to be used on each problem. Finally, Newell and Simon specified the problem-solving strategy in sufficient detail to be programmed in their General Problem Solver.

It seemed to Newell, Simon, and their associates that it would be useful to develop a theoretical approach to problem solving that was relevant to several different kinds of problem rather than to just one. Accordingly, Ernst and Newell (1969) applied the General Problem Solver to 11 rather different problems (e.g. letter-series completion; missionaries and canni- bals; the Tower of Hanoi). They found that the General Problem Solver was able to solve all of the problems. However, it sometimes did not appear to do so in the same way as people.

In their more detailed analysis of problem solving, Newell and Simon (1972) argued that many problems can be represented as a *problem space* consisting of the *initial state* of the problem, the goal state, all of the possible *mental operators* (e.g. moves) that can be applied to any state to change it into a different state, and all of the intermediate states of the problem. From this perspective, the process of problem solving involves a sequence of different *knowledge states*. These knowledge states intervene between the initial state and the goal state, with mental operators produc- ing the shift from one knowledge state to the next.

The above notions can be illustrated if we consider the Tower of Hanoi problem. The initial state of the problem consists of three disks piled in order of size on the first of three pegs. When all of the disks are piled in the same order on the last peg, the goal state has been reached. The rules of the problem specify that only one disk can be moved at a time, and that a larger disk cannot be placed on top of a smaller disk. These rules restrict the possible mental operators on each move. For example, there are only two possible first moves: place the smallest disk on the middle or on the last peg. Each move alters the knowledge state. Some of the knowledge states occurring on the three-peg version of the Tower of Hanoi problem are shown in the figure.

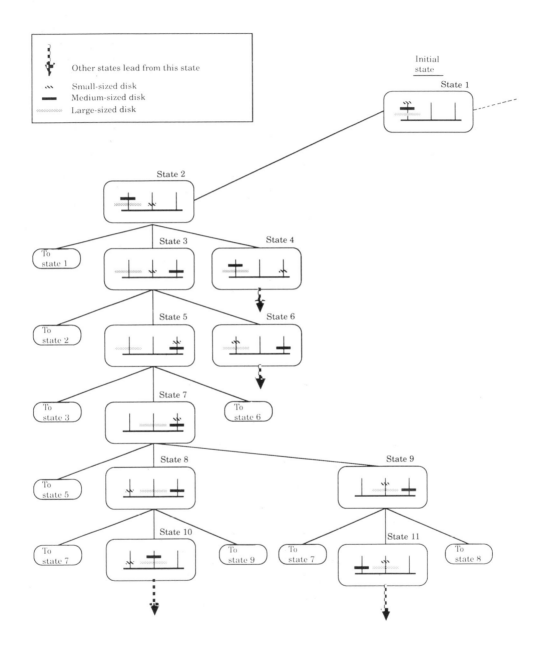

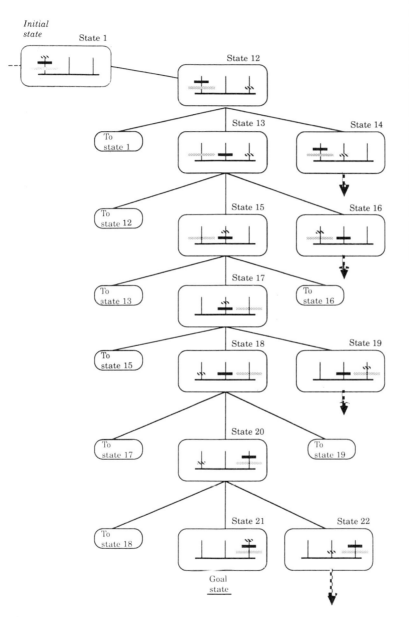

Initial state

State 1

State 12

State 13   State 14

To state 1

To state 12

State 15   State 16

To state 13

State 17   To state 16

To state 15

State 18   State 19

To state 17   To state 19

State 20

To state 18

State 21   State 22

Goal state

A diagram of a portion of the problem space of alternative states that intervene between the initial state and goal state in the Tower of Hanoi problem. The left hand page shows the states arising when the small disk is first moved to the central post (state 2); and on the right hand page are the states following state 12, in which the small disk is first moved to the right hand post.

How do people select mental operators or moves as they proceed from the initial state to the goal state? According to Newell and Simon (1972), the complexity of most problems means that we rely heavily on *heuristic methods*. These are rules of thumb which facilitate the task of thinking about a problem, and which generally enable the problem to be solved. The most important of the various heuristic methods is known as *means-ends analysis*. It consists of the following steps.

- Note the difference between the current state of the problem and the goal state.
- Form a sub-goal that will reduce the difference between the current and goal states.
- Select a mental operator that will permit attainment of the sub-goal.

The way in which means-ends analysis is used can be illustrated with the Tower of Hanoi problem. A reasonable sub-goal in the early stages of the problem is to attempt to place the largest disk on the last peg. If a situation arises in which the largest disk must be placed on either the middle peg or the last peg, then means-ends analysis will lead to that disk being placed on the last peg.

Where means-ends analysis is used extensively, then subjects should tend to experience difficulties if it becomes necessary to make a move that temporarily increases the distance between the current state and the goal state. This prediction was tested by Thomas (1974) using a variant of the missionaries and cannibals problem.

In this problem, three missionaries and three cannibals need to be transported across a river in a boat which can only hold two people. The number of cannibals on either bank of the river must never exceed the number of missionaries, because then the cannibals would eat the missionaries. (In Thomas's (1974) experiment, he used hobbits and orcs, with the orcs wanting to eat the hobbits.) One move involves transferring one cannibal and one missionary back to the starting point, and thus gives the appearance of moving away from the solution (this is the transition between states eight and nine in the problem shown in the figure on page 143). It was at this precise point that the subjects experienced severe difficulties.

Thomas (1974) also obtained evidence that subjects set up sub-goals. He discovered that subjects would frequently carry out a block of several moves at increasing speed, followed by a long pause before embarking on another rapid sequence of moves. This suggested that subjects were dividing the problem up into three or four major sub-goals.

Simon and Reed (1976) considered the learning processes involved in solving a version of the missionaries and cannibals problem in which there

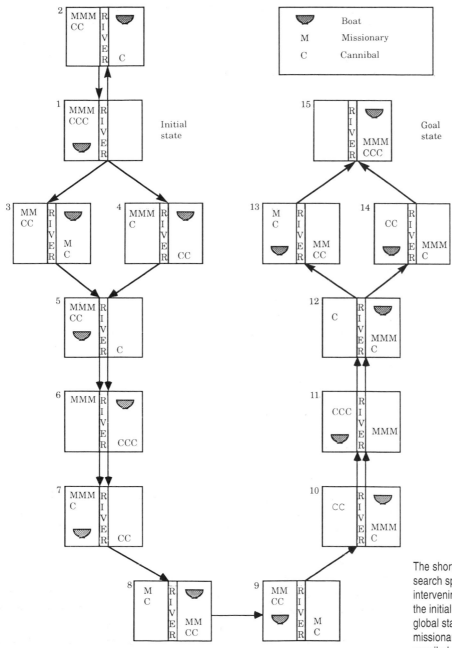

The shortest legal search space intervening between the initial state and global state in the missionaries and cannibals problem.

were five missionaries and five cannibals. Initially, subjects made use of a balancing strategy, in which they endeavoured to have the same number of missionaries and cannibals on each side of the river. However, since this strategy does not enable the problem to be solved, subjects typically shift to a means-ends strategy, in which the primary focus is on moving as many people as possible to the goal-side of the river. Finally, subjects use an anti-looping heuristic designed to avoid moves that have the effect of reversing the immediately preceding move.

According to Simon and Reed (1976), the most important step in learning how to solve the problem is the shift from the balancing strategy to the means-ends strategy. Some subjects were told to reach a state in which three cannibals were on their own on the goal-side of the river. It was hoped that this instruction would reduce reliance on the balancing strategy, and thus speed up problem solution. This was indeed the case. Those given the instruction abandoned the balancing strategy after four moves on average, compared with 15 moves for those not given the instruction.

How successful is the Newell and Simon approach? Basically, it seems to work rather well with well-defined problems in which the initial state, the goal state, and the various permissible moves are all clearly specified. Real life, in contrast, typically confronts us with ill-defined problems that contain many more ambiguities than the problems studied by Newell and Simon (1972).

For example, Eysenck and Keane (1990) refer to the problem of what to do if you lock your keys in your car. It may not be clear whether coat hangers and the police do or do not form part of the initial state. The goal state of gaining access to the car keys and being able to drive away in the car could be achieved by smashing a window, but this solution has obvious disadvantages. It may also be difficult to identify the suitable operators (e.g. is crawling through the boot a viable option?).

The well-defined problems investigated by Newell and Simon (1972) differ from the ill-defined problems of everyday life in other ways. Subjects attempting to solve well-defined problems usually have little specific knowledge about the problem, and so rely on rather general strategies such as means-ends analysis. Solving ill-defined problems, on the other hand, relies much more heavily on possessing the relevant specific knowledge and experience.

The theoretical approach advocated by Newell and Simon (1972) suffers from the limitation that it is only partially applicable to the ill-defined problems we encounter in our lives. On the other hand, their computational approach has proved very successful within the range of problems to which it has been applied.

Reasoning

Philosophers and logicians have often drawn a distinction between *deductive* and *inductive reasoning*. Deductive reasoning is concerned with the conclusions which follow necessarily if certain statements or premises are assumed to be true. It is very important to note that the validity of a given conclusion is based solely on logical principles, and is not affected in any way by whether or not that conclusion is actually true. Thus, for example, if we accept the premises, "If she is a woman, then she is Aristotle", and, "She is a woman", then the conclusion, "She is Aristotle", is valid. The fact that we know that Aristotle was a man is irrelevant to the logical validity of the conclusion.

Inductive reasoning involves making a generalised conclusion from premises that refer to particular instances. For example, from the premise, "Every experiment on learning has found that it depends on reward or reinforcement", one might want to draw the general conclusion, "Learning always depends on reward or reinforcement". This conclusion may seem reasonable, but it is possible that future experiments might demonstrate that there are circumstances in which learning occurs in the absence of reward. In general terms, the conclusions of inductively valid arguments are probably but not necessarily true.

Even though philosophers argue that deductive and inductive reasoning are quite different, is it the case that there are different psychological processes involved in the two kinds of reasoning? To anticipate our future discussion to some extent, we will quote the views of Bolton (1972), who argued as follows:

> Experiments on deductive reasoning show that subjects are influenced sufficiently by their experience for their reasoning to differ from that described by a purely deductive system, whilst experiments on inductive reasoning lead to the view that an understanding of the strategies used by adult subjects in attaining concepts involves reference to higher-order concepts of a logical and deductive nature. [p. 154]

Deductive reasoning

Most research on deductive reasoning has made use of syllogisms, in which a conclusion is drawn from two premises or statements.

Here is an example of a syllogism: "If it is raining then Fred gets wet" and "It is raining" are the two premises, and they permit the valid inference or conclusion, "Fred gets wet". This illustrates one of the most important rules of inference, known as *modus ponens* : given the premise, "If A, then

B", and also given A, one may validly infer B. Another major rule of inference is *modus tollens*: from the premise, "If A, then B", and the premise, "B is false", the conclusion "A is false" necessarily follows. For example, the two premises "If it is raining, then Fred gets wet" and "Fred does not get wet" lead to the conclusion, "It is not raining."

Two other inferences are worth considering at this stage. The first is called *affirmation of the consequent* and the second is called *denial of the antecedent*. Here is an example of affirmation of the consequent:

Premises
If it is raining, then Fred gets wet.
Fred gets wet.
Conclusion
Therefore, it is raining.

Here is an example of denial of the antecedent:

Premises
If it is raining, then Fred gets wet.
It is not raining.
Conclusion
Therefore, Fred does not get wet.

Do you think that these conclusions are valid? Most people argue that they are (Evans, 1989), but in fact they are invalid. In the first instance, affirmation of the consequent, it does not necessarily have to be raining in order for Fred to get wet: he might have jumped into a swimming pool or someone might have turned a hose on him. The same line of reasoning demonstrates why denial of the antecedent is not valid.

We have just seen that deductive reasoning is prone to error when it comes to affirmation of the consequent and denial of the antecedent. The typical finding in experiments on modus ponens and modus tollens is that very few errors are made with modus ponens, but that the error rate often exceeds 30% with modus tollens (Evans, 1989). It is not entirely clear why so many errors are made with modus tollens, but part of the reason is probably that we lack practice in thinking about what is not the case.

The most important theoretical issue is whether or not people think rationally and logically when engaged in deductive reasoning. The existence of numerous errors on most syllogistic reasoning tasks might suggest that people tend to think illogically. However, poor performance could occur for reasons other than illogical thinking. As Mary Henle (1962) pointed out, many errors occur because people misunderstand or misrepresent the problem, even if they then apply logical thinking to it.

Henle (1962) also argued that some errors occur because of the subject's "failure to accept the logical task". This happens if, for example, the subject focuses on the truth or falsity of the conclusion without relating the conclusion to the preceding premises.

Braine, Reiser, and Rumain (1984) have extended and developed Henle's (1962) theoretical approach. According to their natural deduction theory, most of the errors found in deductive reasoning occur because of failures of comprehension. For example, the affirmation of the consequent error occurs because a premise such as "If it is raining, then Fred gets wet" (see above) is interpreted to mean "If Fred gets wet, then it has been raining".

Why should this be so? According to Braine et al. (1984), it is because we normally expect other people to provide us with the information that we need to know. If someone says to you, "If it is raining, then Fred gets wet", it is reasonable to assume that rain is the only event that is likely to make Fred wet.

Braine et al. (1984) obtained some evidence to support their theoretical views. For example, they tried to stop subjects from misinterpreting the premises in affirmation of the consequent syllogisms by providing an additional, clarifying premise along the following lines:

Premises
   If it is raining, then Fred gets wet.
   If it is snowing, then Fred gets wet.
   Fred gets wet
Conclusion
   ?

Subjects were much more likely to argue correctly that there is no valid conclusion when the additional premise was used.

According to Braine et al. (1984), people have a mental rule corresponding to modus ponens. As a result, syllogisms based on modus ponens are easy to handle, and pose no comprehension problems. Byrne (1989) has shown that this is not always true. She presented syllogisms of the following type with the starred premise either present or absent:

Premises
   If she has an essay to write, then she will study late in the library.
   *If the library stays open, then she will study late in the library.
   She has an essay to write.
Conclusion
   ?

Subjects were much less likely to draw the valid modus ponens conclusion (i.e., "She will study late in the library") when the additional (starred) premise was presented. This means that the processes involved in deductive reasoning can be more complex (and probably less logical or rational) than is assumed by natural deduction theory.

There is other evidence indicating that many problems of deductive reasoning occur for reasons other than failures of comprehension. For example, Janis and Frick (1943) discovered that subjects' decisions about the validity of syllogisms depended on their attitude towards the conclusions of those syllogisms. If they agreed with the conclusion, then they tended to say that the syllogism was valid, whereas they claimed that the syllogism was invalid if they did not agree with the conclusion; this is known as *belief bias*. Of course, the personal beliefs of the subjects should have been irrelevant to the issue of whether the conclusion followed logically from the premises, and the fact that their personal beliefs intruded in this way indicates the use of illogical thinking.

There are thus various reasons why deductive reasoning with syllogisms is prone to error. There may be ignorance of some of the rules of inference (e.g. modus tollens), there may be inadequate comprehension of the meanings of the premises, and there may be belief bias. There are other factors at work (see Eysenck & Keane, 1990, for details), but the ones outlined above are perhaps the most important factors in producing errors.

Wason selection task.   A reasoning task which has proved especially useful in shedding light on human thought processes was invented approximately 25 years ago by Peter Wason. It is generally known simply as the Wason selection task. In this task there are four cards lying on a table. Each card has a letter on one side and a number on the other. The subject is told that there is a rule which applies to the four cards (e.g. "If there is an R on one side of the card, then there is a 2 on the other side of the card"). The task is to select only those cards that would need to be turned over in order to decide whether or not the rule is correct.

In one of the most used versions of this selection task, the four cards have the following symbols visible: R, G, 2, and 7, and the rule is the example given (see below). What answer would you give to this problem?

The Wason selection task: "If there is an R on one side of the card, then there is a 2 on the other".

R   G

Most people select either the R card or the R and 2 cards. If you did the same, then you got the answer wrong. The starting point for solving the problem is to recognise that what needs to be done is to see whether any of the cards fail to obey the rule. From this perspective, the 2 card is irrelevant. If there is an R on the other side of it, then all that this tells us is that the rule might be true. If there is any other letter on the other side, then we have also discovered nothing at all about the validity of the rule.

In fact, the correct answer is to select the cards with R and 7 on them—an answer which is selected by only approximately 5% of university students. The reason why the 7 is necessary is that it would definitely disprove the rule if it had an R on the other side. It is of interest to note that there are quite striking similarities between Wason's selection task and syllogistic reasoning. The selection of the 7 card follows from the modus tollens rule of inference: from the premises "If there is an R on one side of the card, then there is a 2 on the other side" and "The 7 card does not have a 2 on it", it follows logically that the 7 card should not have an R on the other side. If it does, then the premise specifying the rule must be incorrect. In other words, poor performance on the Wason selection task is due in part to the general difficulty that people have with making the modus tollens inference.

Several researchers have argued that the abstract nature of the task makes it difficult to solve. Wason and Shapiro (1971) used four cards (Manchester, Leeds, car, and train) and the rule, "Every time I go to Manchester I travel by car". Again the task is to select only those cards that need to be turned over to prove or disprove the rule. The correct answer that the Manchester and train cards need to be turned over was given by 62% of the subjects, against only 12% when the Wason selection task was given in its abstract form.

It might appear from the findings of Wason and Shapiro (1971) that the use of concrete and meaningful material on the Wason task facilitates the reasoning process. Difficulties for this view emerged from a study by Griggs and Cox (1982), however. They used the same tasks as Wason and Shapiro (1971) with American students in Florida. They failed to find a greater success rate for the meaningful task, presumably because most American students have no direct experience of Manchester or Leeds.

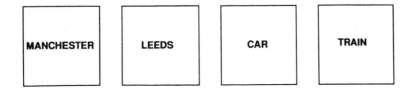

The concrete version of Wason's selection task.

Seventy-three per cent of the same students produced the correct answer when the rule corresponded to the Florida law on drinking and was related to their own experience. The rule stated that: "If a person is drinking beer, then the person must be over 19 years of age."

The findings of Griggs and Cox (1982) led them to propose a memory cueing hypothesis, according to which people need specific prior experience before they can perform well on the Wason selection task. Results obtained by Griggs and Cox (1983), however, cast doubt on the memory-cueing hypothesis. Subjects were asked to imagine that they were Sears' store managers responsible for checking sales receipts, and the rule to be tested was, "If a purchase exceeds $30, then the receipt must be approved by the department manager." In spite of the fact that the subjects had no direct experience of checking sales receipts, approximately 70% of them solved the problem correctly.

How can we account for the findings of Griggs and Cox (1983)? One possibility is that the subjects made use of relevant past experience, even though they had never worked as store managers. Another possibility is that people use relatively abstract rules, called *pragmatic reasoning schemata* by Cheng and Holyoak (1985). According to these psychologists, we are regularly exposed to situations involving permission (e.g. in order to gain permission to enter university, it is necessary to achieve certain examination results) and obligation (e.g. if there is an accident, then the appropriate person in authority must be informed). As a result of this exposure, we have learned pragmatic reasoning schemata or rules that allow us to solve versions of the Wason task that involve permission or obligation. The existence of such rules based on obligation led to the high performance obtained by subjects in the study by Griggs and Cox (1983).

Mental models.   A new and important theoretical approach to deductive reasoning has been proposed by Phil Johnson-Laird (1983). He proposed that we should stop arguing that thinking is logical when it succeeds and illogical when it fails. Instead, we should say that successful thinking results from the use of appropriate mental models and unsuccessful thinking occurs when we make use of inappropriate mental models.

A mental model is simply a representation of the state of affairs described in the premises of a problem, and it may be in the form of imagery. This representation depends on the way in which the premises are interpreted. The construction of a mental model can be illustrated with the following examples taken from Eysenck and Keane (1990):

Premises

The lamp is on the right of the pad.
The book is on the left of the pad.
The clock is in front of the book.
The vase is in front of the lamp.

Conclusion

The clock is to the left of the vase.

According to Johnson-Laird (1983), people use the information contained in the premises to construct a mental model like this:

book	pad	lamp
clock		vase

It is easy to see from this model that the conclusion that the clock is to the left of the vase is valid. In many cases, however, there will be more than one mental model which is consistent with the premises:

Premises

The lamp is on the right of the pad.
The book is on the left of the lamp.
The clock is in front of the book.
The vase is in front of the pad.

Conclusion

The clock is to the left of the vase.

Mental model one

book	pad	lamp
clock	vase	

Mental model two

pad	book	lamp
vase	clock	

Someone who constructed only mental model one would mistakenly conclude that the clock is to the left of the vase. It would be clear to someone who constructed both mental models, on the other hand, that the clock is not necessarily to the left of the vase.

The key features of Johnson-Laird's theory of mental models can be summarised as follows:

- Comprehension of the premises of a problem leads to the construction of one or more mental models representing the state of affairs indicated by the premises.

- The model or models that have been constructed are used to produce a novel conclusion not directly specified in the premises.
- There is a check to decide whether there are any additional models of the premises which invalidate the novel conclusion.
- The above three processes all depend on the processing resources of working memory (see Chapter 4), and thus can be affected by its limited capacity; in particular, errors are likely to occur when several mental models have to be constructed and held in working memory.

Evidence that the limited capacity of working memory can lead to errors in reasoning was obtained by Johnson-Laird (1983). He asked his subjects to indicate what conclusions followed validly from sets of premises, and varied the demands on working memory by manipulating the number of mental models that were consistent with the premises. Seventy-eight per cent of subjects drew the valid conclusion when the premises only allowed the generation of one mental model, but this figure dropped to 29% when two mental models were possible, and to 13% with three mental models.

Inductive reasoning: concept learning

Much of the research on inductive reasoning has been concerned with concept learning. What is a concept? According to Bourne (1966), a concept exists "whenever two or more distinguishable objects or events have been grouped or classified together, and set apart from other objects on the basis of some common feature or property characteristic of each."

Probably the best known research on concept learning was carried out by Bruner, Goodnow, and Austin (1956). They used stimuli consisting of rectangular cards picturing various shapes. These cards varied in four dimensions or attributes: number of borders around the edges of the cards (one, two, or three); number of shapes in the middle of the cards (one, two, or three); the shapes themselves (square, circle, or cross); and colour of the shapes (red, black, or green). The concepts used by Bruner et al. (1956) were typically conjunctive concepts, in which a number of features must be present together in order for a card to be positive (e.g. "three black circles"). In many of their studies, they employed a *selection paradigm*. The subjects had all of the cards in front of them, and selected one at a time. They were not told what the concept was. After each selection, they were informed whether or not they had chosen a positive instance of the concept. The subjects were allowed at any point to offer hypotheses as to the concept that the experimenter had in mind.

One of the advantages of the selection paradigm is that the pattern of selections made by each subject allows the experimenter to infer the problem-solving strategies used during concept learning. It appeared that subjects mainly used a rather limited number of different strategies. One was conservative focusing. This involves focusing on the first positive instance, and then selecting another card that differs from it in only one attribute. If this second card is also a positive instance, then the attribute which changed is clearly irrelevant to the concept. Thus, for example, if one green circle with three borders is a positive instance, and so is one green circle with two borders, then the number of borders does not form part of the concept. However, if the second card is a negative instance, then the attribute which varied is part of the concept.

A related strategy, but one that is rather riskier, is focus gambling. This involves altering two or more of the attributes of the first positive instance when selecting the next card. A rather different kind of strategy is successive scanning. Subjects using this strategy begin with a specific hypothesis, which they then attempt to test by selecting cards that will provide useful information.

Bruner et al. (1956) discovered that focusing was generally more successful than scanning, in the sense that fewer cards needed to be selected before the concept was identified. A particular problem with scanning is that it can make substantial demands on memory, and so produce what Bruner et al. referred to as "cognitive strain". This was shown clearly in a study in which the first two concept problems were solved with the set of stimulus cards in sight, but the third problem had to be solved without looking at the cards, and so imposed an extra memory load. The result was that scanners took longer to solve the third problem than the first two, whereas focusers were unaffected by the increased memory load.

Bruner et al. (1956) also carried out experiments on concept learning using what they termed the *reception paradigm*, in which the experimenter rather than the subject decided on the sequence of positive and negative instances to be presented. With this paradigm, most subjects used either a wholist or a partist strategy. In the wholist strategy, all of the features of the first positive instance are taken as the hypothesis. Any of these features that are not present in subsequent positive instances are eliminated from the hypothesis. In contrast, the partist strategy involves taking part of the first positive instance as a hypothesis. After that, the original hypothesis is maintained provided that the subject consistently makes correct decisions about positive and negative instances. When a mistake is made, subjects following the partist strategy try to choose a new hypothesis that is consistent with the information obtained from previous cards.

The wholist strategy was generally more effective than the partist strategy. Wholist subjects only needed to remember the current hypothesis, and could ignore information about previous instances, whereas partist subjects had to remember information from all of the cards. Approximately twice as many subjects used the wholist strategy as used the partist strategy in the studies of Bruner et al. (1956), but other researchers using different concepts have typically found that the partist strategy is used much more frequently than the wholist strategy. Whether the wholist or partist strategy is adopted depends on factors such as the cognitive skills of the individual and the complexity of the problem.

While the approach to concept learning adopted by Bruner et al. (1956) is important, it can be criticised on a number of grounds. We will consider two of the main criticisms here:

- First, decisions about the strategies used by the subjects were not made in a precise fashion. For example, it was often argued that subjects had employed a particular strategy in spite of the fact that several of their selections differed from those that would have been expected using that strategy (e.g. choosing cards that provided no new information).

- Second, it is not entirely clear that the findings have much relevance to everyday life. Focusing is highly efficient in a task with a very small number of potentially relevant attribute dimensions, such as the one used by Bruner et al. (1956). In the real world, however, focusing would usually only permit an individual to eliminate dimensions one by one from an almost infinite set. And while the laboratory subject can afford the luxury of suspending judgement about the nature of the concept while focusing on one attribute dimension after another, the same person in everyday life may need to decide rapidly whether to approach or to avoid another person or an object. In such circumstances, the appropriate strategy is to act on the basis of the best available hypothesis, as happens with the scanning strategy.

An interesting approach to concept learning resembling the selection paradigm of Bruner et al. (1956) was initiated by Peter Wason (1960). He told his subjects that the three numbers 2 4 6 conformed to a simple relational rule. Their task was to generate sets of three numbers, and to provide reasons for each choice. After each choice, the experimenter indicated whether or not the set of numbers conformed to the rule that the experimenter had in mind. The subjects' task was to discover what the rule was. As the rule was apparently a very simple one, namely, "three numbers in ascending order of magnitude", one might imagine that most of the subjects would have solved it rather quickly. In fact, only 21% of the subjects were correct with their first attempt to state the rule.

Performance on Wason's relational rule problem was so poor because most of the subjects thought of a hypothesis that was too specific (e.g. the second number is twice the first, and the third number is three times the first), and then generated sets of numbers that were consistent with that hypothesis (e.g. 6 12 18; 50 100 150). Because their original hypothesis was constantly confirmed, subjects following this strategy tended to assume that it must be correct. In fact, the best way of testing the correctness of a hypothesis is to look for sets of numbers that will *disconfirm* the hypothesis. For example, someone whose hypothesis was that the first number was double the second and the third number was three times the first could have attempted to disconfirm it by selecting the set of numbers, 8 14 48. This set is consistent with the actual relational rule, but is not consistent with the hypothesis being considered. In essence, failure to attempt hypothesis disconfirmation prevented the subjects from replacing their initial hypotheses, which were too narrow and specific, with the correct general rule.

Further evidence that subjects are reluctant to look for disconfirming evidence in this concept learning task was obtained by Wason (1968). Sixteen subjects announced their hypotheses, and were then asked what they would do in order to ascertain whether their hypotheses were incorrect. Three of them defiantly insisted that their hypotheses could not possibly be incorrect, and nine others said that they would generate only sets of numbers that were consistent with their hypothesis. Only four of the subjects gave the correct answer, which is to generate sets of numbers inconsistent with the hypothesis.

Prototype theory.   In recent years, there has been increased interest in the kinds of concepts which we all use in everyday life. According to Mervis and Rosch (1981), most concepts are rather untidy and can be regarded as imprecise or "fuzzy". Clear illustrations of the imprecision of some concepts were obtained by McCloskey and Glucksberg (1978). They asked 30 people whether a "stroke" was a disease: 16 said it was, and 14 said it was not. Exactly the same result was obtained when the same people were asked whether a "pumpkin" was a fruit. More surprisingly, when McCloskey and Glucksberg tested the same subjects a month later, 11 had changed their minds about a stroke being a disease, and eight had changed their minds about a pumpkin being a fruit.

Why are so many concepts fuzzy in nature? Several theorists, including Mervis and Rosch (1981), have proposed prototype theories in which each concept is organised around a *prototype*, a set of characteristic features. The decision as to whether or not a particular instance is regarded as a member of a given concept or category is determined by the number of characteristic features of that concept which it possesses. A pumpkin possesses some (but by no means all) of the characteristic features of a fruit, and so many people are not sure whether it should be regarded as a fruit or not.

We can see more clearly how this kind of prototype theory works by considering the concept "bird". This concept has having wings, the ability to fly, having feathers, and relatively small as some of its characteristic features. Birds, such as the robin, which possess most of the characteristic features are regarded as "better" or more typical birds than those, such as the ostrich, which do not. Some birds, such as the penguin, lack a number of the characteristic features of most birds, and because of this we often forget that they are actually birds.

According to prototype theory, two members of a concept or category do not have to have exactly the same features. Indeed, it might even happen that two members belonging to the same category have no features at all in common. Such extreme flexibility in terms of category membership can be seen in Wittgenstein's (1958) discussion of the concept of "games":

> Consider for example the proceedings that we call "games". I mean board-games, card-games, ball-games, Olympic games, and so on. What is common to them all ... if you look at them you will not see something that is common to all, but similari-

ties, relationships, and a whole series of them at that ... Look for example at board-games, with their multifarious relationships. Now pass to card-games; here you will find many correspondences with the first group, but many common features drop out, and others appear. When we pass next to ball-games, much that is common is retained, but much is lost ... Is there always winning and losing, or competition between players? Think of patience. In ball-games there is winning and losing; but when a child throws his ball at the wall and catches it again, this feature has disappeared.[pp. 31-32].

There is evidence that prototypes play an important role in learning and memory. For example, Franks and Bransford (1971) constructed prototypes by combining geometric forms such as circles, stars, and triangles into structured groupings. Several distortions of these prototypes were subsequently formed by applying one or more transformations to them. Subjects were then shown some of these distorted patterns (but not the prototypes themselves), followed by a recognition test which included the prototypes.

The results were quite striking (see the figure below). The subjects were most confident that they had seen the prototype, in spite of the fact that

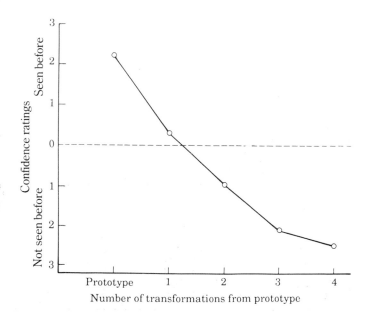

Recognition memory for geometric forms varying in their similarity to the prototype, defined by the number of transformations from the prototype. None of the forms had actually been presented before. (Data from Franks and Bransford).

the prototypes had not been shown to them at all. In fact, they had seen examples of the other kinds of patterns, although not the exact stimuli presented on the recognition test.

Those patterns differing from a prototype by a single transformation were the next most confidently recognised, and there was a straightforward relationship between the degree of similarity of a pattern to its prototype and recognition confidence. What these findings suggest is that the subjects formed prototypes during the initial learning (which corresponded to those which the experimenter started with) and stored them in long-term memory. This prototype knowledge was then used to classify and identify new stimuli, with recognition being simply a function of the extent to which any given pattern matched the stored prototype.

While prototype theories have proved rather successful, it should be noted that theorists disagree among themselves about the exact nature of the underlying prototypes. Some theorists (e.g. Mervis & Rosch, 1981) argue that a prototype is rather abstract and is represented by characteristic features. Other theorists (e.g. Hintzman & Ludlum, 1980) argue that the prototype is more concrete and consists of the best member (or small set of best members) of the concept. Thus, for example, the prototype of the furniture category might be "chair" or a set of items of furniture (e.g. chair, table, bed). It remains unclear which of these theoretical approaches is closer to the truth.

Most versions of prototype theory are better able to account for relatively concrete categories or concepts than for more abstract ones. Hampton (1981) examined a range of abstract concepts. While some of these concepts (e.g. a work of art, a science or a crime) appeared to have prototypes, other abstract concepts (e.g. a rule or a belief) did not. One reason why it is not possible to identify a prototype for such concepts may be that the range of possible rules and beliefs is too wide for the entire category to be represented by a set of characteristic features.

Decision making and judgement

Thinking frequently involves making a decision about the best choice to be made from a set of alternatives. Decision making can therefore be identified as an important topic within the general field of thinking. Decision making in most situations involves considering the *values* of the possible outcomes of different choices and of the *probabilities* of those outcomes occurring. For example, consider the decision of which subject to study at university. Each possible choice carries with it value implications for future employment prospects in terms of the range of jobs which might be available, the degree of interest associated with each job, the rate of pay for each job, and so on. The probability or likelihood of getting any of these jobs will vary according to which subject is studied at university, and so probabilities need to be considered as well as values.

Normative and empirical decision making

It is useful to distinguish between *normative* and *empirical decision making*. Studies of normative decision making are concerned with identifying the best or most rational ways of making decisions, and have been used extensively in economics. In contrast, empirical studies involve a consideration of the processes actually used by people grappling with complex decisions. Wright (1984) has discussed the normative multi-attribute utility approach, which can be used when one out of a number of objects has to be chosen. According to this approach, the decision maker should identify dimensions relevant to the decision, decide how to weight these dimensions, obtain a total utility (i.e. usefulness) for each object by summing its weighted dimensional values, and then select the object with the highest weighted total. The evidence suggests that this approach is rarely adopted in practice, presumably because of the demands that it would place on the processing system.

As Gilhooly (1990) pointed out, there are some plausible theoretical accounts of how decision making is actually carried out. For example, Tversky (1972) proposed an *elimination-by-aspects* theory, and Simon (1978) put forward a *satisficing* theory. According to Tversky (1972), the decision maker eliminates options by considering one relevant attribute after another. For example, someone buying a house may first of all consider the attribute of geographical location, eliminating from consideration all those houses not lying within a given area. He or she may then consider the attribute of price, eliminating all those properties costing above a given figure. This process continues attribute by attribute until there is only one option remaining. While this is a reasonably undemanding strategy, it suffers from the limitation that the option selected can vary as a function of the order in which the attributes are considered. This means that often the best choice will not be made. Simon's (1978) satisficing theory is particularly appropriate when the various options become available at different points in time. An example here would be the vexed issue of choosing someone to marry. According to the theory, decision makers set a minimum acceptable level, and the first option which reaches that level is selected. If the initial level of acceptability is set too high or too low, it can be adjusted upwards or downwards to make it more realistic.

"NUMBER TWO...TURN TO THE RIGHT, PLEASE...."

It is reasonably clear that the actual way in which people make decisions depends importantly on the nature of the decision and on the personality and other characteristics of the person making the decision. However, a generalisation which is often true is that decision makers use a combination of the techniques discussed above. For example, Payne (1976) investigated the ways in which subjects chose a flat or apartment from information presented on cards. Most subjects initially used techniques such as elimination by aspects and satisficing in order to reduce the possibilities to manageable proportions, and then considered the remaining possibilities in a more thorough fashion corresponding to the dictates of multi-attribute utility theory.

Judgements of probability

The judged probability of events is of major importance in decision making. As a consequence, considerable research in recent years has focused on the processes involved in making probability judgements, and on the errors that can occur.

Suppose, for example, that you read in a medical encyclopaedia that a physical complaint from which you are suffering is one of the symptoms of a relatively rare and unpleasant disease. Suppose further that one person in 500 has the disease, that the probability of having the physical symptom if you are suffering from the disease is 0.7, and that the probability of having the symptom without also having the disease is 0.01. Most people in those circumstances would argue that there was a high probability that they were suffering from the disease. In actual fact, however, the correct probability is only 0.123.

Why is our judgement of probability so far out in this case? In general terms, it has been argued by Kahneman and Tversky (1973) that people decide between various possibilities (e.g., having versus not having the disease) by considering which possibility seems to be most representative of, or consistent with, the evidence (e.g., having a physical complaint). What tends to be left out of account is the *base-rate information*, which in the case we have been discussing refers to the relative numbers of people suffering from, and not suffering from, the disease. Since the number of non-sufferers is vastly greater than the number of sufferers, this reduces greatly the probability that a person with the physical symptom will actually be suffering from the disease.

According to Kahneman and Tversky (1973), when people are asked to make probability judgements, they often resort to the *representativeness heuristic*. This is a rule of thumb, according to which representative or typical instances of a category are judged to be more probable than unrepresentative ones. For example, you are told three facts about a man—he is unscrupulous, dishonest, and wants to be Prime Minister. Do you think it is more likely that he is a politician or a railwayman? Probably you feel it is more likely that he is a politician, because his characteristics appear to be more representative or typical of politicians than of railwaymen. However, there are very many more workers for British Rail than there are politicians, and so it is actually more likely that he is a railwayman.

Kahneman and Tversky (1973) illustrated the use of the representativeness heuristic with a task in which subjects were told that descriptions of people had been selected at random from a set of 100 descriptions. Half the subjects were told that 70 of the people described were engineers and 30 were lawyers. The other half were told that there were 70 lawyers and 30 engineers. After the subjects had read each description, they had to indicate the probability of the person described being an engineer or lawyer.

One of the descriptions was as follows: "Dick is a 30-year-old man. He is married with no children. A man of high ability and high motivation, he promises to be quite successful in his field. He is well liked by his colleagues" (p. 242). This description seems to be equally close to the stereotyped views of what lawyers and engineers are like, and so use of the representativeness heuristic would lead to the decision that there was a 0.5 probability that Dick was a lawyer or an engineer.

That is exactly what most of the subjects decided. However, this decision ignores the base-rate information, according to which the actual numbers of lawyers and engineers are quite different. Kahneman and Tversky (1973) discovered that base-rate information was used sometimes. When the subjects were told that a description had been chosen at random, but were not given the description, then they estimated the probability that the person was an engineer was either 0.7 or 0.3, depending on the base-rate information that had been supplied. In this case the representativeness heuristic could not be used. What we have here is the intriguing situation that base-rate information is used when no information is provided, but is totally ignored when worthless information is provided!

Tversky and Kahneman (1983) have produced even more striking evidence of the kinds of error that can result from using the representativeness heuristic. In particular, they observed what they called the *conjunction fallacy*. For example, subjects might be told that an imaginary person called Linda is a former student activist, single, very intelligent, and a philosophy graduate. They are then asked to estimate the probabilities of her being a bank teller, a feminist, or a feminist bank teller. Most subjects say that it is much more probable that Linda is a feminist bank teller than a bank teller. This cannot be correct, because the category of bank tellers obviously includes all feminist bank tellers.

Are there circumstances in which people do not rely on the representativeness heuristic and instead make proper use of base-rate information? According to Tversky and Kahneman (1980), base-rate information is much more likely to be used when its causal relevance to the probability to be judged is emphasised. They told their subjects that there were two taxi companies in a town; these were the Blue Company and the Green Company. An accident involving a taxi occurred, and the subjects' task was to decide the probability that the taxi had been blue. Some subjects were told that 50% of the taxis in the town were blue and the remaining 50% green, but that 85% of the taxi-related accidents involved green taxis. They were also told that a witness said that a blue taxi was involved, but there was a 20% chance that he was mistaken.

Since the causal relevance of the base-rate information (i.e. the percentage of accidents caused by blue taxis) was made obvious, subjects relied heavily on that information in assessing the likelihood that the taxi involved in the accident was blue, getting close to the correct figure of 59%.

Other subjects were simply told that 85% of the taxis were blue and 15% green, with no mention being made of the relevance of this information to accident causation. These subjects largely ignored the base-rate information, and relied instead on the eywitness evidence. Most of these subjects claimed mistakenly that there was an 80% probability that the taxi was blue.

Tversky and Kaheman (1973) investigated another heuristic or rule of thumb known as the *availability heuristic*, according to which probability judgements are sometimes made on the basis of how available relevant examples are in long-term memory. They asked their subjects whether each of five letters of the alphabet (K, L, N, R, and V) occurs more often in the first or the third position in English words. In spite of the fact that all five letters appear in the third position in more words than they do in the first position, subjects tended to argue that each letter actually appears in the first position of more words. The reason for these errors in judging probabilities probably revolves around the representativeness heuristic: it is much easier to generate words starting with a given letter than those having the same letter in the third position.

You may be wondering why it is that people use the representativeness and availability heuristics when both strategies can lead to errors in thinking. Part of the reason is that these heuristics are often reasonably accurate. For example, if people were asked to estimate the relative frequencies of words beginning with L and with N, or with L and N in the third position, then it is very likely that differences in the availability of relevant words would reflect differences in actual frequency. If you were asked whether someone was more likely to be an engineer or a lawyer, and there were equal numbers of engineers and lawyers, then it would be entirely appropriate to make use of the representativeness heuristic in providing an answer. The characteristics of a sample generally resemble those of the category from which the sample comes, and the representativeness heuristic incorporates that insight. When the representativeness heuristic produces errors, it usually does so because other factors are ignored, rather than because the representativeness heuristic is irrelevant.

The other main reason why people resort to heuristics is because they reduce cognitive strain by offering a straightforward way of tackling many diverse problems. Most people are not expert statisticians, and so find it difficult to combine several different kinds of information into an accurate probability judgement. The representativeness and availability heuristics provide a simple method of making such judgements.

Summary: Thinking

- Problem solving has been investigated in a number of different ways. Past experience can sometimes have adverse effects on problem solving. Studies of expertise have revealed that experts perform better than non-experts because they have a far greater store of relevant knowledge. There is increasing evidence that they also possess superior strategic skills. Attempts to produce computer programs that will mimic human problem solving have suggested that people often rely on heuristic methods, which are convenient rules of thumb.

- Research on reasoning can be divided into work concerned with deductive reasoning, in which certain conclusions follow necessarily from given premises, and work concerned with inductive reasoning, in which the conclusions are never more than probable. It has been claimed by some theorists that people reason logically on deductive reasoning tasks, and that errors are largely due to lack of comprehension of the premises. Other theorists have argued that most thinking is illogical. The most promising theoretical approach is based on the assumption that people form mental models representing the state of affairs indicated by the premises, and that the validity or otherwise of any conclusions are assessed based on those mental models.

- Much of the research on inductive reasoning has been concerned with concept learning. This research has indicated that there are various different strategies that subjects typically use in concept learning tasks. Work on inductive reasoning has also indicated that subjects are generally reluctant to look for evidence that might disconfirm their hypotheses. There is increasing evidence to indicate that most concepts are organised around prototypes or sets of characteristic features, and that learning often leads to the storage of prototype knowledge.

- Research on decision making has shown that empirical or actual decision making differs in various ways from normative decision making, which is based on an entirely rational approach. More specifically, elimination by aspects and satisficing are often found in empirical decision making, even though these strategies cannot be guaranteed to produce the best solution. Judgements of probability are frequently required in decision making. There are various heuristics or rules of thumb which are used in the production of probability judgements. One example is the representativeness heuristic. This involves making decisions on the basis of the extent to which the features of an object or individual are representative of, or similar to the features that are characteristic of some cateogory. Heuristics often lead to reasonably accurate performance, and have the advantage of minimising cognitive strain. However, there are circumstances in which the use of heuristics has been found to lead to extremely inaccurate judgements.

Further reading

The various topics dealt with in this chapter are discussed more fully in M.W. Eysenck and M.T. Keane (1990), *Cognitive Psychology: A Student's Handbook* (Hove, U.K.: Lawrence Erlbaum Associates Ltd.). There are several interesting chapters on different aspects of thinking, including a particular emphasis on the computational or cognitive science approach, in K.J. Gilhooly (Ed.) (1989), *Human and Machine Problem Solving* (London: Plenum).

References

Adams, R.J., Maurer, D., & Davis, M. (1986). Newborns' discrimination of chromatic from achromatic stimuli. *Journal of Experimental Child Psychology, 41,* 267–281.

Allport, D.A. (1980). Attention and performance. In G. Claxton (Ed.), *Cognitive psychology: New directions.* London: Routledge.

Allport, D.A., Antonis, B., & Reynolds, P. (1972). On the division of attention: A disproof of the single channel hypothesis. *Quarterly Journal of Experimental Psychology, 24,* 225–235.

Anderson, J.R. (1980). *Cognitive psychology and its implications.* San Francisco: W.H. Freeman.

Anderson, R.C. & Pichert, J.W. (1978). Recall of previously unrecallable information following a shift in perspective. *Journal of Verbal Learning and Verbal Behavior, 17,* 1–12.

Atkinson, R.C. & Shiffrin, R.M. (1968). Human memory: A proposed system and its control processes. In K.W. Spence and J.T. Spence (Eds.), *The psychology of learning and motivation, vol. 2.* London: Academic Press.

Baddeley, A.D. & Hitch, G. (1974). Working memory. In G.H. Bower (Ed.), *The psychology of learning and motivation, vol. 8.* London: Academic Press.

Bard, E.G., Shillcock, R.C., & Altmann, G.T.M. (1988). The recognition of words after their acoustic offsets in spontaneous speech: Effects of subsequent context. *Perception and Psychophysics, 29,* 191–211.

Bartlett, F.C. (1932). *Remembering: A study in experimental and social psychology.* Cambridge: Cambridge University Press.

Beauvois, M.F. & Derousne, J. (1979). Phonological alexia: Three dissociations. *Journal of Neurology, Neurosurgery and Psychiatry, 42,* 1115–1124.

Beck, I.L. & Carpenter, P.A. (1986). Cognitive approaches to understanding reading. *American Psychologist, 41,* 1088–1105.

Bernstein, B. (1973). *Class, codes and control.* London: Paladin.

Blakemore, C. (1975). Central visual processing. In M.S. Gazzaniga and C. Blakemore (Eds.), *Handbook of psychobiology.* London: Academic Press.

Boden, M. (1988). *Computer models of the mind.* Cambridge: Cambridge University Press.

Bolton, N. (1972). *The psychology of thinking.* London: Methuen.

Bourne, L.E. (1966). *Human conceptual behavior.* Boston: Allyn & Bacon.

Bower, G.H., Black, J.B., & Turner, T.J. (1979). Scripts in memory for text. *Cognitive Psychology, 11,* 177–220.

Bower, T.G.R. (1964). Discrimination of depth in premotor infants. *Psychonomic Science, 1,* 368.

Bower, T.G.R., Broughton, J.M., & Moore, M.K. (1970). The co-ordination of visual and tactual input in infants. *Perception and Psychophysics, 8,* 51–53.

Braine, M.D.S., Reiser, B.J., & Rumain, B. (1984). Some empirical justification for a theory of natural propositional logic. In G.H. Bower (Ed.), *The psychology of learning and motivation, vol. 18.* New York: Academic Press.

Bransford, J.D. (1979). *Human cognition: Learning, understanding and remembering.* Belmont, CA: Wadsworth.

Bransford, J.D., Barclay, J.R., & Franks, J.J. (1972). Sentence memory: A constructive versus interpretive approach. *Cognitive Psychology, 3,* 193–209.

Bransford, J.D. & Johnson, M.K. (1972). Contextual prerequisites for understanding: Some investigations of comprehension and recall. *Journal of Verbal Learning and Verbal Behavior, 11*, 717–726.

Broadbent, D.E. (1958). *Perception and communication.* London: Pergamon.

Broadbent, D.E. (1971). *Decision and stress.* London: Academic Press.

Brown, R., Cazden, C.B., & Bellugi, U. (1969). The child's grammar from I to III. In J.P. Hill (Ed.), *Minnesota symposium on child psychology, vol. 2.* Minneapolis: University of Minnesota Press.

Bruner, J.S. (1957). On perceptual readiness. *Psychological Review, 64,* 123–152.

Bruner, J.S., Goodnow, J.J., & Austin, G.A. (1956). *A study of thinking.* New York: Wiley.

Bruner, J.S. & Postman, L. (1949). On the perception of incongruity: A paradigm. *Journal of Personality, 18,* 206–223.

Bub, D., Cancelliere, A., & Kertesz, A. (1985). Whole-word and analytic translation of spelling to sound in a non-semantic reader. In K.E. Patterson, J.C. Marshall, & M. Coltheart (Eds.), *Surface dyslexia: Neuropsychological and cognitive studies of phonological reading.* Hove, UK: Erlbaum Ltd.

Byrne, R.M.J. (1989). Suppressing valid inferences with conditionals. *Cognition, 31,* 61–83.

Carmichael, L. M., Hogan, H.P., & Walter, A.A. (1932). An experimental study of the effect of language on the reproduction of visually perceived forms. *Journal of Experimental Psychology, 15,* 73–86.

Carpenter, P.A. & Daneman, M. (1981). Lexical retrieval and error recovery in reading: A model based on eye fixations. *Journal of Verbal Learning and Verbal Behavior, 20,* 137–160.

Cheng, P. & Holyoak, K.J. (1985). Pragmatic reasoning schemas. *Cognitive Psychology, 17,* 391–416.

Cherry, E.C., (1953). Some experiments on the recognition of speech with one and two ears. *Journal of the Acoustical Society of America, 25,* 975–979

Chomsky, N. (1957). *Syntactic structures.* The Hague: Mouton.

Chomsky, N. (1965). *Aspects of the theory of syntax.* Cambridge, Mass.: MIT Press.

Cohen, G. (1989). *Memory in the Real World.* Hove: Lawrence Erlbaum Associates Ltd.

Cohen, N.J. (1984). Preserved learning capacity in amnesia: Evidence for multiple memory systems. In L.R. Squire and N. Butters (Eds.), *Neuropsychology of memory.* New York: Guilford Press.

Collins, A.M. & Loftus, E.F. (1975). A spreading-activation theory of semantic processing. *Psych. Review, 82,* 407–428.

Collins, A.M. & Quillian, M.R. (1969). Retrieval time from semantic memory. *Journal of Verbal Learning and Verbal Behavior, 9,* 432–438.

Craik, F.I.M. & Lockhart, R.S. (1972). Levels of processing: A framework for memory research. *Journal of Verbal Learning and Verbal Behavior, 11,* 671–684.

Daneman, M. & Carpenter, P.A. (1980). Individual differences in working memory and reading. *Journal of Verbal Learning and Verbal Behavior, 19,* 450–466.

De Groot, A.D. (1966). Perception and memory versus thought. In B. Kleinmuntz (Ed.), *Problem solving.* New York: Wiley.

Dell, G.S. (1986). A spreading-activation theory of retrieval in sentence production. *Psychological Review, 93,* 283–321.

Deutsch, J.A. & Deutsch, D. (1963). Attention: Some theoretical considerations. *Psychological Review, 70,* 80–90.

Duncan, J. (1979). Divided attention: The whole is more than the sum of its parts. *Journal of Experimental Psychology: Human Perception, 5,* 216–228.

Duncker, K. (1945). On problem solving. *Psychological Monographs, 58, No. 5 (Whole No. 270),* 1–113.

Ellis, A.W. & Young, A.W. (1988). *Human cognitive neuropsychology.* Hove, UK: Lawrence Erlbaum Associates Ltd.

Ernst, G.W. & Newell, A. (1969). *GPS: A case study in generality and problem solving.* London: Academic Press.

Evans, J. St. B.T. (1989). *Bias in human reasoning.* Hove, UK: Erlbaum Ltd.

Eysenck, M.W. (1977). *Human memory: Theory, research and individual differences.* Oxford: Pergammon.

Eysenck, M.W. (1979). Depth, elaboration, and distinctiveness. In L.S. Cermak and F.I.M. Craik (Eds.), *Levels of processing in human memory.* Hillsdale, NJ: Lawrence Erlbaum Associates Inc.

Eysenck, M.W. (1982a). *Attention and arousal: Cognition and performance.* Berlin: Springer.

Eysenck, M.W. (1982b). Incidental learning and orienting tasks. In C.R. Puff (Ed.), *Handbook of research methods in human memory and cognition.* London: Academic Press.

Eysenck, M.W. (1984). *A handbook of cognitive psychology.* Hove: Erlbaum Ltd.

Eysenck, M.W. (1988). Individual differences, arousal, and monotonous work. In J.P. Leonard (Ed.), *Vigilance: Methods, models, and regulation.* Frankfurt: Lang.

Eysenck, M.W. & Keane, M.T. (1990). *Cognitive psychology: A student's handbook.* Hove, UK: Lawrence Erlbaum Associates Ltd.

Fantz, R.L. (1961). The origin of form perception. *Scientific American, 204,* 66–72.

Fantz, R.L. (1966). Pattern discrimination and selective attention as determinants of perceptual development from birth. In A.H. Kidd and J.F. Rivoire (Eds.), *Perceptual development in children.* New York: International Universities Press.

Fechner, G. (1860). *Elemente der Psychophysik.* Berlin: Springer.

Franks, J.J. & Bransford, J.D. (1971). Abstraction of visual patterns. *Journal of Experimental Psychology, 90,* 65–74.

Garrett, M.F. (1976). Syntactic processes in sentence production. In R.J. Wales and E. Walker (Eds.), *New approaches to language mechanisms.* Amsterdam: North Holland.

Garrett, M.F. (1984). The organization of processing structures for language production: Applications to aphasic speech. In D. Caplan, A.R. Lecours, and A. Smith (Eds.), *Biological perspectives on language.* Cambridge, Mass.: MIT Press.

Gauld, A. & Stephenson, G.M. (1967). Some experiments relating to Bartlett's theory of remembering. *British Journal of Psychology, 58,* 39–50.

Ghiseli, B. (1952). *The creative process.* New York: Mentor.

Gibson, E.J. (1969). *Principles of perceptual learning and development.* New York: Appleton-Century-Crofts.

Gibson, E.J., Shapiro, F., & Yonas, A. (1968). Confusion matrices of graphic patterns obtained with a latency measure. The analysis of reading skill: A program of basic and applied research. *Final report project No. 5–1213,* Cornell University.

Gibson, E.J. & Walk, R.D. (1960). The visual cliff. *Scientific American, 202,* 64–71.

Gibson, J.J. (1979). *The ecological approach to visual perception.* Boston: Houghton Mifflin.

Gick, M.L. & Holyoak, K.J. (1980). Analogical problem solving. *Cognitive Psychology, 12,* 306–355.

Gilhooly, K.J. (1989). *Human and machine problem solving.* London: Plenum.

Gilhooly, K.J. (1990). Decision making and judgement. In M.W. Eysenck (Ed.), *The Blackwell dictionary of cognitive psychology.* Oxford: Blackwell.

Gomulicki, B.R. (1956). Recall as an abstractive process. *Acta Psychologica, 12,* 77–94.

Gould, J.D. (1978). An experimental study of writing, dictating and speaking. In J. Requin (Ed.), *Attention and performance, vol. VII.* Hillsdale, NJ: Erlbaum Inc.

Gould, J.D. (1979). Writing and speaking letters and messages. *IBM Research Report, RC-7528.*

Gould, J.D. (1980). Experiments on composing letters: Some facts, some myths, and some observations. In L.W. Gregg & E.R. Sternberg (Eds.), *Cognitive processes in writing.* Hillsdale, NJ: Erlbaum Inc.

Graf, P. & Schachter, D.L. (1985). Implicit and explicit memory for new associations in normal and amnesic subjects. *Journal of Experimental Psychology: Learning, Memory, and Cognition, 11,* 501–518.

Graf, P., Squire, L.R., & Mandler, G. (1984). The information that amnesic patients do not forget. *Journal of Experimental Psychology: Learning, Memory, and Cognition, 10,* 164–178.

Graf, R. & Torrey, J.W. (1966). Perception of phrase structure in written language. *American Psychological Association Convention Proceedings,* 83–88.

Greene, J. (1986). *Language understanding: A cognitive approach.* Milton Keynes: Open University Press.

Gregory, R.L. (1970). *The intelligent eye.* New York: McGraw-Hill.

Gregory, R.L. (1972). Seeing as thinking. *Times Literary Supplement, June 23.*

Griggs, R.A. & Cox, J.R. (1982). The elusive thematic-material effect in Wason's selection task. *British Journal of Psychology, 73,* 407–420.

Griggs, R.A. & Cox, J.R. (1983). The effects of problem content and negation on Wason's selection task. *Quarterly Journal of Experimental Psychology, 35A,* 519–533.

Hampton, J.A. (1981). An investigation of the nature of abstract concepts. *Memory and Cognition, 9,* 149–156.

Harris, M. & Coltheart, M. (1986). *Language processing in children and adults: An introduction to psycholinguistics.* London: Routledge & Kegan Paul.

Hayes, J.R. & Flower, L.S. (1986). Writing research and the writer. *American Psychologist, 41,* 1106–1113.

Hayes, J.R., Flower, L.S., Schriver, K., Stratman, J., & Carey, L. (1985). *Cognitive processes in revision* (Tech. Rep. No. 12). Pittsburgh, PA: Carnegie Mellon Univ.

Heider, E. (1972). Universals in colour naming and memory. *Journal of Experimental Psychology, 93,* 10–20.

Henle, M. (1962). On the relation between logic and thinking. *Psychological Review, 69,* 366–378.

Herriot, P. (1969). The comprehension of active and passive sentences as a function of pragmatic expectations. *Journal of Verbal Learning and Verbal Behavior, 8,* 166–169.

Hintzman, D.L. & Ludlum, G. (1980). Differential forgetting of prototypes and old instances: Simulation by an exemplar-based classification model. *Memory and Cognition, 8,* 378–382.

Hockey, G.R.J., MacLean, A., & Hamilton, P. (1981). State changes and the temporal patterning of component resources. In J. Long and A. Baddeley (Eds.), *Attention and performance, vol. IX.* Hillsdale: Erlbaum Inc.

Holding, D.H. (1989). Adversary problem solving by humans. In J.J. Gilhooly (Ed.), *Human and machine problem solving.* London: Plenum.

Holding, D.H. & Reynolds, J.R. (1982). Recall or evaluation of chess positions as determinants of chess skill. *Memory and Cognition, 10,* 237–242.

Holmes, D.S. (1972). Repression or interference: A further investigation. *Journal of Personality and Social Psychology, 22,* 163–170.

Hubel, D.H. & Wiesel, T.N. (1962). Receptive fields, binocular interaction and functional architecture in the cat's visual cortex. *Journal of Physiology, 160,* 106–154.

Humphrey (1951). *Thinking: An introduction to its experimental psychology.* London: Methuen.

Humphreys, G.W. & Bruce, V. (1989). *Visual cognition.* Hove, UK: Erlbaum Ltd.

Hyde, T.S. & Jenkins, J.J. (1973). Recall for words as a function of semantic, graphic, and syntactic orienting tasks. *Journal of Verbal Learning and Verbal Behavior, 12,* 471–480.

James, W. (1890). *Principles of psychology.* New York: Holt.

Janis, I.L. & Frick, F. (1943). The relationship between attitudes towards conclusions and errors in judging logical validity of syllogisms. *Journal of Experimental Psychology, 33,* 73–77.

Johnson-Laird, P.N. (1983). *Mental models.* Cambridge: Cambridge University Press.

Johnson-Laird, P.N. & Stevenson, R. (1970). Memory for syntax. *Nature, 227,* 412.

Johnston, W.A. & Dark, V.J. (1985). Dissociable domains of selective processing. In M.I. Posner and O.S.M. Marin (Eds.), *Mechanisms of attention: Attention and performance, vol. XI.* Hillsdale: Erlbaum Inc.

Johnston, W.A. & Dark, V.J. (1986). Selective

attention. *Annual Review of Psychology, 37,* 43–75.

Johnston, W.A. & Heinz, S.P. (1978). Flexibility and capacity demands of attention. *Journal of Experimental Psychology: General, 107,* 420–435.

Johnston, W.A. & Heinz, S.P. (1979). Depth of non-target processing in an attention task. *Journal of Experimental Psychology, 5,* 168–175.

Kahneman, D. & Henik, A. (1979). Perceptual organisation and attention. In M. Kubovy and J.R. Pomerantz (Eds.), *Perceptual organization.* Hillsdale: Erlbaum Inc.

Kahneman, D. & Tversky, A. (1973). On the psychology of prediction. *Psychological Review, 80,* 237–251.

Kaufer, D., Hayes, J.R., & Flower, L.S. (1986). Composing written sentences. *Research in the Teaching of English, 20,* 121–140.

Keenan, J.M., MacWhinney, B., & Mayhew, D. (1977). Pragmatics in memory: A study of natural conversation. *Journal of Verbal Learning and Verbal Behavior, 16,* 549–560.

Kinchla, R.A. & Wolf, J.M. (1979). The order of visual processing: "Top-down," "bottom-up," or "middle-out." *Perception and Psychophysics, 25,* 225–231.

Kintsch, W. & Keenan, J. (1973). Reading rate and retention as a function of the number of propositions in the base structure of sentences. *Cognitive Psychology, 5,* 257–274.

Koffka, K. (1935). *Principles of Gestalt psychology.* New York: Harcourt Brace.

Kohler, W. (1925). *The mentality of apes.* New York: Harcourt Brace, & World.

Kolers, P.A. (1972). *Aspects of motion perception.* New York: Pergamon.

LaBerge, D. (1983). Spatial extent of attention to letters and words. *Journal of Experimental Psychology: Human Perception and Performance, 9,* 371–379.

Lachman, R., Lachman, J.L., & Butterfield, E.C. (1979). *Cognitive psychology and information processing.* Hillsdale: Erlbaum Inc.

Latour, P.L. (1962). Visual threshold during eye movements. *Vision Research, 2,* 261–262.

Lenneberg, E.H. & Roberts, J.M. (1956). *The language of experience.* Memoir 13. University of Indiana, Publications in Anthropology and Linguistics.

Levine, D.N., Calvanio, R., & Popovics, A. (1982). Language in the absence of inner speech. *Word, 15,* 19–44.

Levine, M. (1971). Hypothesis theory and non-learning despite ideal S-R reinforcement contingencies. *Psychological Review, 78,* 130–140.

Levine, M.W. & Schefner, J.M. (1981). *Fundamentals of sensation and perception.* London: Addison-Wesley.

Ley, P. (1978). Memory for medical information. In M.M. Gruneberg, P.E. Morris, and R.N. Sykes (Eds.), *Practical aspects of memory.* London: Academic Press.

Lieberman, P. (1963). Some effects of semantic and grammatical context on the production and perception of speech. *Language and Speech, 6,* 172–187.

Loftus, E.F. & Loftus, G.R. (1980). On the permanence of stored information in the human brain. *American Psychologist, 35,* 409–420.

Logan, G.D. (1988). Toward an instance theory of automatisation. *Psychological Review, 95,* 492–527.

Luchins, A.S. (1942). Mechanisation in problem solving: The effect of Einstellung. *Psychological Monographs, 54* (248).

Mackworth, N.H. (1950). Researches in the measurement of human performance. *Medical Research Council Special Report, Series 268.*

Mandler, G. (1967). Organisation and memory. In K.W. Spence and J.T. Spence (Eds.), *The psychology of learning and motivation: Advances in research and theory, vol. 1.* London: Academic Press.

Marr, D. (1982). Vision: *A computational investigation into the human representation and processing of visual information.* San Francisco: W.H. Freeman.

Marr, D. & Nishihara, K. (1978). Representation and recognition of the spatial organization of three-dimensional shapes. *Philosophical Transactions of the Royal Society (London), B200,* 269–294.

Marslen-Wilson, W. & Tyler, L.K. (1980). The temporal structure of spoken language understanding. *Cognition, 8,* 1–71.

McCloskey, M.E. & Glucksberg, S. (1978). Natural categories: Well defined or fuzzy sets? *Memory and Cognition, 6,* 462–472.

McGurk, H. & MacDonald, J. (1976). Hearing lips and seeing voices. *Nature, 264,* 746–748.

McLeod, P. (1977). A dual task response modality effect: Support for multiprocessor models of attention. *Quarterly Journal of Experimental Psychology, 29,* 651–667.

Mervis, C.B. & Rosch, E. (1981). Categorisation of natural objects. *Annual Review of Psychology, 32,* 89–115.

Miller, G.A. (1956). The magic number seven, plus or minus two: Some limits on our capacity for processing information. *Psychological Review, 63,* 81–93.

Miller, G.A. & McNeill, D. (1969). Psycholinguistics. In G. Lindzey and E. Aronson (Eds.), *The handbook of social psychology, vol. III.* Reading, Mass.: Addison-Wesley.

Morris, C.D., Bransford, J.D., & Franks, J.J. (1977). Levels of processing versus transfer appropriate processing. *Journal of Verbal Learning and Verbal Behavior, 16,* 519–533.

Morris, P.E. (1979). Strategies for learning and recall. In M.M. Gruneberg and P.E. Morris (Eds.), *Applied problems in memory.* London: Academic Press.

Morris, P.E., Jones, S., & Hampson, P. (1978). An imagery mnemonic for the learning of people's names. *British Journal of Psychology, 69,* 335–336.

Mullin, J. & Corcoran, D.W.J. (1977). Interaction of task amplitude with circadian variation in auditory vigilance performance. *Ergonomics, 20,* 193–200.

Nachreiner, F. (1977). Experiments on the validity of vigilance experiments. In R.R. Mackie (Ed.), *Vigilance: Theory, operational performance, and physiological correlates.* London: Plenum.

Navon, D. (1977). Forest before trees: The precedence of global features in visual perception. *Cognitive Psychology, 9,* 353–383.

Neisser, U. (1976). *Cognition and reality.* San Francisco: Freeman.

Newell, A. & Simon, H.A. (1972). *Human problem solving.* Englewood Cliffs: Prentice-Hall.

Norman, D.A. & Bobrow, D.G. (1975). On data-limited and resource-limited processes. *Cognitive Psychology, 7,* 44–64.

Osgood, C.E. (1953). *Method and theory in experimental psychology.* Oxford: Oxford University Press.

Palincsar, A.S. & Brown, A.L. (1984). Reciprocal teaching of comprehension-fostering and comprehension-monitoring activities. *Cognition and Instruction, 1,* 117–175.

Parkin, A.J. (1982). Residual learning in organic amnesia. *Cortex, 18,* 417–440.

Payne, J. (1976). Task complexity and contingent processing in decision making: An information search and protocol analysis. *Organizational Behavior and Human Performance, 16,* 366–387.

Penfield, W. (1969). Consciousness, memory, and man's conditioned reflexes. In K. Pribram (Ed.), *On the biology of learning.* New York: Harcourt, Brace, & World.

Pullman, S.G. (1987). Computational models of parsing. In A.W. Ellis (Ed.), *Progress in the psychology of language, vol. 3.* Hove, UK: Erlbaum Ltd.

Putnam, B. (1979). Hypnosis and distortions in eyewitness memory. *International Journal of Clinical and Experimental Hypnosis, 27,* 437–448.

Rayner, K. & Pollatsek, A. (1987). Eye movements in reading: A tutorial review. In M. Coltheart (Ed.), *Attention and performance, vol. XII.* Hove, UK: Erlbaum Ltd.

Reason, J.T. (1979). Actions not as planned. In G. Underwood & R. Stevens (Eds.), *Aspects of consciousness.* London: Academic Press.

Reason, J.T. & Mycielska, K. (1982). *Absent minded? The psychology of mental lapses and everyday errors.* Englewood Cliffs, NJ: Prentice-Hall.

Roediger, H.L. (1980). Memory metaphors in cognitive psychology. *Memory & Cognition, 8,* 231–246.

Roth, I. & Frisby, J. (1986). *Perception and rep-*

resentation: A cognitive approach. Milton Keynes: Open University Press.

Rumelhart, D.E. (1977). Introduction to human information processing. Chichester: Wiley.

Rumelhart, D.E. & Norman, D.A. (1983). Representation in memory. In R.C. Atkinson, R.J. Herrnstein, B. Lindzey, & R.D. Luce (Eds.), Handbook of experimental psychology. Chichester: Wiley.

Scardamalia, M. & Bereiter, C. (1987). Written composition. In M. Wittrock (Ed.), Third handbook of research on testing. New York: Macmillan.

Schneider, W. & Shiffrin, R.M. (1977). Controlled and automatic human information processing: I. Detection, search and attention. Psychological Review, 84, 1–66.

Segal, S.J. & Fusella, V. (1970). Influence of imaged pictures and sounds on detection of visual and auditory signals. Journal of Experimental Psychology, 83, 458–464.

Shallice, T. & Warrington, E.K. (1970). Independent functioning of verbal memory stores: A neuropsychological study. Quarterly Journal of Experimental Psychology, 22, 261–273.

Shiffrin, R.M. & Schneider, W. (1977). Controlled and automatic human information processing: II. Perceptual learning, automatic attending, and a general theory. Psychological Review, 84, 127–190.

Silveira, J. (1971). Incubation: The effect of interruption timing and length on problem solution and quality of problem processing. Unpublished Ph.D. thesis, University of Oregon.

Simon, H.A. (1974). How big is a chunk? Science, 183, 482–488.

Simon, H.A. (1978). Rationality as process and product of thought. American Economic Association, 68, 1–16.

Simon, H.A. & Gilmartin, K. (1973). A simulation of memory for chess positions. Cognitive Psychology, 5, 29–46.

Simon, H.A. & Reed, S.K. (1976). Modelling strategy shifts on a problem solving task. Cognitive Psychology, 8, 86–97.

Sinclair-de-Zwart, H. (1969). Developmental psycholinguistics. In D. Elkind and J.

Flavell (Eds.), Studies in cognitive development. Oxford: Oxford University Press.

Slater, A.M. (1990). Perceptual development. In M.W. Eysenck (Ed.), The Blackwell dictionary of cognitive psychology. Oxford: Blackwell.

Smith, S.M., Brown, H.O., Toman, J.E.P., & Goodman, L.S. (1947). Lack of cerebral effects of D-tubocurarine. Anaesthesiology, 8, 1–14.

Spelke, E.S., Hirst, W.C., & Neisser, U. (1976). Skills of divided attention. Cognition, 4, 215–230.

Stevens, S.S. (1951). Mathematics, measurement and psychophysics. In S.S. Stevens (Ed.), Handbook of experimental psychology. Chichester: Wiley.

Sullivan, L. (1976). Selective attention and secondary message analysis: A reconsideration of Broadbent's filter model of selective attention. Quarterly Journal of Experimental Psychology, 28, 167–178.

Thomas, J.C. (1974). An analysis of behaviour in the hobbits-orcs problem. Cognitive Psychology, 6, 257–269.

Thorndike, E.L. (1898). Animal intelligence: An experimental study of the associative processes in animals. The Psychological Review Monograph Supplements, 2, No. 4 (Whole No. 8).

Treisman, A.M. (1964). Verbal cues, language, and meaning in selective attention. American Journal of Psychology, 77, 206–219.

Treisman, A.M. (1988). Features and objects: The 14th Bartlett Memorial Lecture. Quarterly Journal of Experimental Psychology, 40A, 201–237.

Treisman, A.M. & Gelade, G. (1980). A feature-integration theory of attention. Cognitive Psychology, 12, 97–136.

Treisman, A.M. & Schmidt, H. (1982). Illusory conjunctions in the perception of objects. Cognitive Psychology, 14, 107–141.

Tulving, E. (1972). Episodic and semantic memory. In E. Tulving and W. Donaldson (Eds.), Organisation of memory. London: Academic Press.

Tulving, E. (1974). Cue-dependent forgetting. American Scientist, 62, 74–82.

Tulving, E. (1979). Relation between encoding specificity and levels of processing. In L.S. Cermak & F.I.M. Craik (Eds.), Levels of processing in human memory. Hillsdale: Erlbaum Inc.

Tulving, E. & Pearlstone, Z. (1966). Availability versus accessibility of information in memory for words. *Journal of Verbal Learning and Verbal Behavior, 5,* 381–391.

Tversky, A. (1972). Elimination by aspects: A theory of choice. *Psychological Review, 79,* 281–299.

Tversky, A. & Kahneman, D. (1973). Availability: A heuristic for judging frequency and probability. *Cognitive Psychology, 5,* 207–232.

Tversky, A. & Kahneman, D. (1980). Causal schemas in judgements under uncertainty. In M. Fishbein (Ed.), *Progress in social psychology.* Hillsdale, NJ: Erlbaum Inc.

Tversky, A. & Kahneman, D. (1983). Extensional versus intuitive reasoning: The conjunction fallacy in probability judgement. *Psychological Review, 90,* 293–315.

Underwood, G. (1974). Moray vs. the rest: The effect of extended shadowing practice. *Quarterly Journal of Experimental Psychology, 26,* 368–372.

van Dijk, T.A. & Kintsch, W. (1983). *Strategies of discourse comprehension.* London: Academic Press.

von Senden, M. (1932). *Space and sight: The perception of space and shape in the congenitally blind before and after operation.* London: Methuen.

von Wright, J.M., Anderson, K., & Stenman, U. (1975). Generalization of conditioned GSRs in dichotic listening. In P.M.A. Rabbitt and S. Dornic (Eds.), *Attention and Performance, vol. V.* London: Academic Press.

Vygotsky, L.S. (1934). *Thought and language.* Cambridge, Mass.: MIT Press.

Wallas, G. (1926). *The art of thought.* London: Cape.

Warm, J.S., Epps, B.D., & Ferguson, R.P. (1974). Effects of knowledge of results and signal regularity on vigilance performance. *Bulletin of the Psychonomic Society, 4,* 272–274.

Warren, R.M. & Warren, R.P. (1970). Auditory illusions and confusions. *Scientific American, 223,* 30–36.

Wason, P.C. (1960). On the failure to eliminate hypotheses in a conceptual task. *Quarterly Journal of Experimental Psychology, 12,* 129–140.

Wason, P.C. (1968). Reasoning about a rule. *Quarterly Journal of Experimental Psychology, 20,* 273–281.

Wason, P.C. & Shapiro, D. (1971). Natural and contrived experience in reasoning problems. *Quarterly Journal of Experimental Psychology, 23,* 63–71.

Watkins, M.J. (1974). When is recall spectacularly higher than recognition? *Journal of Experimental Psychology, 102,* 161–163.

Weiskrantz, L. (1986). *Blindsight: A case study and its implications.* Oxford: Oxford University Press.

Weist, R.M. (1972). The role of rehearsal: Recopy or reconstruct? *Journal of Verbal Learning and Verbal Behavior, 11,* 440–445.

Wertheimer, M. (1962). Psychomotor co-ordination of auditory-visual space at birth. *Science, 134,* 1692.

Whorf, B.L. (1956). *Language, thought, and reality.* Cambridge, Mass.: MIT Press.

Wilkins, A.J. (1976). A failure to demonstrate effects of the retention interval. Cited in J.E. Harris, Remembering to do things: A forgotten topic, in J.E. Harris & P.E. Morris (Eds.), *Everyday memory, actions and absentmindedness.* London: Academic Press.

Wilkins, A.J. & Baddeley, A.D. (1978). Remembering to recall in everyday life: An approach to absentmindedness. In M.M. Gruneberg, P.E. Morris, and R.N. Sykes (Eds.), *Practical aspects of memory.* London: Academic Press.

Wittgenstein, L. (1958). *Philosophical investigations.* New York: Macmillan.

Wright, G. (1984). *Behavioural decision theory.* Harmondsworth: Penguin.

Glossary

Absolute threshold: the least intense stimulus in a given modality which can be detected; see Differential threshold.

Affirmation of the consequent: an invalid inference in syllogistic reasoning which is commonly made.

Affordances: the various possible uses of objects (e.g. being sat on is an affordance of a chair), which according to James Gibson are given directly in the sensory information provided by the stimulus.

Anticipation error: a mistake in speech in which a word is spoken earlier in the sentence than it should be; this form of error is usually taken as evidence of forward planning in speech production.

Automatic processing: processing which typically occurs rapidly, does not require attention, and for which there is no conscious awareness; automatic processes generally develop as a result of prolonged practice.

Availability heuristic: a rule-of-thumb strategy used in making probability judgements (e.g. does the letter R occur in the first or the third position in more English words?), in which the availability of relevant examples in long-term memory determines the judgement.

Belief bias: a source of error in reasoning in which people decide whether the conclusion of a syllogism is valid on the basis of whether or not they agree with it.

Binaural task: an auditory task in which two messages are presented at the same time to both ears; it is used to study attention.

Binocular disparity: the two eyes receive slightly different views of an object; this facilitates depth perception, especially when the object is relatively close.

Bottom-up processing: see Stimulus-driven processing.

Categorical clustering: the tendency for a categorised list of words presented in random order to be recalled category by category; illustrates organisational factors in memory.

Central capacity interference theory: the view that the ability to perform two tasks at the same time depends on the demands which those tasks place on some common central capacity (e.g. attention; effort); generally regarded as over-simplified because more specific capacities are ignored.

Closed-loop mode of control: this form of control over behaviour involves attentional mechanisms and the use of feedback from behaviour; it usually leads to accurate performance, and can be contrasted with Open-loop mode of control (q.v.).

Cochlea: a part of the ear and thus involved in auditory perception; there is a cochlea in each ear, consisting of a coiled tube filled with liquid.

Cognitive neuropsychologists: psychologists who attempt to understand human cognition through the study of brain-damaged patients whose cognitive functioning is impaired.

Complex cells: cells in the visual cortex which respond maximally to lines having a given orientation; see Simple cells.

Conceptually driven processing: processing which is affected by an individual's knowledge and expectations rather than by stimulus-driven processing.

Cones: receptors in the retina (mostly in the central area) which are of use in colour vision and in making fine discriminations; see also Rods.

Conjunction fallacy: an error in probability judgements in which people are unduly influenced by the representativeness heuristic (q.v.).

Constancy: the tendency to perceive accurately the characteristics of objects (e.g. colour; sise; shape) across wide variations of presentation in terms of distance, orientation, lighting, and so on.

Convergence: with both eyes fixating the same object, they need to turn inwards to a greater extent when the object is close to than if it is further away; this provides a useful cue to distance with nearby objects.

Cue-dependent forgetting: forgetting which occurs because of the lack of a suitable retrieval cue; see also Trace-dependent forgetting.

Declarative knowledge: knowledge in long-term memory which is concerned with knowing that; this form of knowledge encompasses episodic memory (q.v.) and semantic memory (q.v.), and can be contrasted with procedural knowledge (q.v.).

Deductive reasoning: a form of reasoning in which definite conclusions follow provided that certain statements are assumed to be true; illustrated by syllogistic reasoning.

Deep structure: that which reflects the underlying meaning of a sentence in the theoretical position of Noam Chomsky; to be contrasted with surface structure.

Denial of the antecedent: a relatively common error in syllogistic reasoning in which an invalid conclusion is accepted as valid.

Dichotic listening task: a task used in attention research in which one auditory message is presented to one ear and a different auditory message is presented to the other ear.

Differential threshold: the smallest change in a given stimulus which is detectable; see Absolute threshold.

Dissociation: normal performance on one task but severely impaired performance on a second task in a brain-damaged patient; many dissociations occur because the two tasks make use of different modules (q.v.); see also Double dissociation.

Distinctiveness: as applied to memory, the extent to which a memory trace is unique or dissimilar to other memory traces; distinctive memory traces tend to be well remembered.

Divided attention: an experimental situation in which subjects attempt to perform two different tasks at the same time.

Double dissociation: normal performance on one task coupled with severely impaired performance on a second task by some brain-damaged patients, together with exactly the opposite pattern of performance shown by other brain-damaged patients; double dissociations are often regarded as providing powerful evidence for the existence of modules (q.v.)

Echoic store: a limited-capacity store in the auditory modality in which information can be held for about two seconds after the presentation of an auditory stimulus.

Ecological validity: the extent to which the findings of psychological research are applicable to the "real" world and to everyday life.

Elaborated code: a complex and abstract form of language production which is readily understood, and which Bernstein claimed was used much more by middle-class than by working-class children; see also Restricted code.

Elaboration: as applied to memory, the amount of information of a particular kind which is incorporated into the memory trace; elaborated memory traces are generally better remembered than non-elaborated ones.

Empirical decision making: the process people confronting complex problems actually use to arrive at decisions.

Encoding specificity principle: a notion proposed by Endel Tulving, according to which remembering depends on the amount of overlap between the information contained in the memory trace and that available in the retrieval environment.

Episodic memory: long-term memory for autobiographical or personal events, usually including some information about the time and the place of a particular episode or event; see also Declarative knowledge and Semantic memory.

Exchange error: an error in speech production in which two words in a sentence are switched around, this type of error is often taken as evidence of forward planning in speech production.

Explicit memory: memory which involves the conscious recollection of previous occurrences; see also Implicit memory.

False alarm: as applied to vigilance research, a report that a signal has been presented when in fact it has not.

Feature integration theory: proposed by Anne Treisman, claiming that the perception of an object requires focused attention in order to combine the features of that object.

Feature theories: theories of pattern recognition in which it is assumed that the features or distinctive parts of a stimulus are extracted at an early stage of perception.

Feedback mode of control: see Closed-loop mode of control.

Fenestra ovalis: a part of the ear involved in auditory perception; more specifically, an opening in the bone which surrounds the inner ear.

Focused attention: an experimental situation in which subjects attempt to attend to only one source of stimulation while ignoring other stimuli.

Functional fixedness: a limitation in problem solving in which subjects focus on only very possible functions or uses of objects and ignore other, more unusual, uses.

Gestalt: literally "organised whole", but the word is generally used to refer to a school of psychology that emphasised the importance of organisation in perception.

Grapheme-phoneme conversion rules: rules which determine the relationship between the written and spoken forms of words; there are many exceptions to these rules in the English language.

Heuristic methods: applied to problem solving and decision making, they are rules of thumb which facilitate problem solving, but sometimes at the expense of accuracy.

Hypercomplex cells: cells in the visual area of the cortex which respond maximally to lines of a given length.

Hypothesis set: the pool of possible answers considered by a subject engaged in problem solving.

Iconic store: a limited-capacity store in the visual modality in which information can be held for about half a second after the presentation of a visual stimulus.

Image displacement: shifting position of the image of an object on the retina, which can provide useful information about the movement of objects.

Immediacy assumption: the assumption that virtually all of the processes involved in language comprehension are carried out as soon as each word in a sentence is presented rather than being delayed to the end of the phrase or the sentence.

Implicit memory: memory which does not require the conscious recollection of past experiences; far more of our memory is implicit than used to be assumed; see also Explicit memory.

Induced movement: an illusory effect, in which an object which is not actually moving appears to be moving because of the movement of surrounding objects (e.g. a stationary train at a station when an adjacent train starts moving).

Inductive reasoning: a form of reasoning in which a generalised conclusion is drawn from specific information; the conclusion cannot be shown to be necessarily true.

Inference drawing: a process involved in comprehension, in which missing information in the linguistic message is guessed at on the basis of relevant knowledge.

Initial state: in Newell and Simon's theory, the starting point for problem solving.

Knowledge state: in Newell and Simon's theory, each discrete problem position which occurs between the initial state (q.v.) and the goal state.

Knowledge-telling strategy: an approach in writing often used by children in which they put down their knowledge on a topic in an unorganised fashion; see also Knowledge-transforming strategy.

Knowledge-transforming strategy: an approach to writing used by skilled writers, in which knowledge of possible problems with writing permits the devising of an effective writing plan; see also Knowledge-telling strategy.

Law of Praganz: the notion espoused by the Gestalt (q.v.) school of psychology that perception will usually be as psychologically organised as possible.

Levels-of-processing theory: an approach to memory proposed by Craik and Lockhart in which it was argued that long-term memory depends on the extent to which learning involves the processing of meaning.

Linguistic competence: within Noam Chomsky's theory of language, the abstract knowledge of language possessed by people; see also Linguistic performance.

Linguistic performance: within Noam Chomsky's theory of language, the actual imperfect language performance of individuals, which can be contrasted with linguistic competence (q.v.).

Linguistic relativity: the viewpoint, proposed by Benjamin Lee Whorf and others, that thinking is determined by language; weaker versions of this viewpoint assume that language has a strong influence on thinking.

Macropropositions: general propositions formed during the process of story comprehension which serve to identify its macrostructure (q.v.).

Macrostructure: the overall gist or structure of a story which is comprehended by listeners to, or readers of, a story after macropropositions (q.v.) have been formed.

Magnitude estimation: a method for assessing the intensity or magnitude of sensations in which numbers are assigned to stimuli on the basis of the apparent magnitudes of the sensations produced.

Means-ends analysis: a method used in problem solving identified by Newell and Simon in which an attempt is made to reduce the difference between the current position on a problem and the desired goal position.

Mental models: used in reasoning to provide one or more representations of the state of affairs suggested in the premises; the precise form of representation (e.g. imaginal) is typically not known.

Mental operators: in the theory of problem solving proposed by Newell and Simon, the complete set of possible moves which permit the problem solver to move from the initial state (q.v.) to the goal state.

Misapplied size-constancy theory: a theory used to account for many of the visual illusions, it assumes that the processes producing size constancy (see Constancy) with three-dimensional objects may be used wrongly in the perception of two-dimensional objects.

Modules: independent or nearly independent specific processes within the cognitive system; cognitive neuropsychologists (q.v.) claim to have identified numerous different modules.

Modus ponens: one of the key rules of syllogistic inference, according to which the conclusion "B is true" follows from the premises "A is true" and "if A, then B"; see Modus tollens.

Modus tollens: one of the key rules of syllogistic inference, according to which the conclusion "A is false" follows from the premises "If A, then B" and "B is false"; many errors are made with this rule, as Wason discovered with his selection task.

Movement after-effect: illusory movement in the opposite direction to previously seen real movement; probably due to reduced sensitivity in the cells responding to the real movement.

Motion parallax: objects beyond the point of fixation appear to be moving in the opposite direction to objects closer than the point of fixation to a moving observer; this phenomenon is of use in establishing the distance of objects.

Multi-store model of memory: the view that there are three different kinds of memory store: modality-specific stores; short-term store; and long-term store.

Negative afterimages: the perception of colours complementary to those just seen in a bright stimulus; these afterimages depend on reduced cone (q.v.) sensitivity and increased firing of non-stimulated cones.

Negative transfer effect: as applied to problem solving, an interfering or disruptive effect of previous problem solving on a current problem.

Open-loop mode of control: a form of control involving motor programs or other automatic processing (q.v.), used mainly following extensive practice; undue reliance on this mode of control is found in absentmindedness.

Optic flow patterns: perceptual effect experienced by someone moving rapidly (e.g. a pilot), in which the visual environment appears to move away from the point towards which he or she is moving; this effort can be used by pilots to provide useful information about their direction, speed, and altitude.

Oscilloscope: an instrument for producing a representation of a rapidly changing quantity on the screen of a cathode-ray tube.

Ossicles: three bones in the ear between the tympanic membrane (q.v.) and the fenestra ovalis.

Parallel processing: two or more cognitive processes occurring at the same time; see Serial processing.

Perceptual differentiation: the notion put forward by Eleanor and James Gibson that perceptual development in children involves an improved ability to identify the key features of stimuli.

Perceptual enrichment hypothesis: the notion that children's perceptual development involves supplementing the available sensory information with a growing store of relevant knowledge.

Perceptual span: as applied to reading, the maximum number of letters from which useful information can be extracted; estimates of the size of the perceptual span vary, but are mostly in the range of 15–20 letters.

Phonemic restoration effect: the finding with auditory presentation of sentences that subjects use conceptually driven processing (q.v.) to "fill in" a missing phoneme.

Phonology: the rules governing the sound system of a language.

Positive transfer effect: as applied to problem solving, the finding that performance on a current problem benefits from previous problem solving.

Pragmatic reasoning schemata: rules relating to permission and obligation which (according to Cheng & Holyoak, 1985) are used to facilitate solution of reasoning problems.

Primal sketch: the initial stage of perceptual processing in which information about basic features (e.g. edges; contours) is represented; see also Three-dimensional model representation and Two-point-five-dimensional sketch.

Primary memory: short-term memory or the psychological present; a term introduced into psychology by William James.

Proactive interference: as applied to memory, the finding that current learning and memory are disrupted by previous learning; it is generally greatest when the stimuli in the two learning tasks are the same but the responses are different; see also Retroactive interference.

Problem space: in the theory of Newell and Simon, it consists of the initial stage (q.v.) of a problem, the solution of goal state, and the complete set of mental operators (q.v.).

Procedural knowledge: knowledge relating to knowing how, and including motor skills; memory for such knowledge is typically revealed by skilful performance and not by conscious recollection; see also Declarative knowledge.

Prospective memory: memory for actions which need to be performed in the future (e.g. make travel arrangements for a holiday); see also Retrospective memory.

Prototype: a set of features characteristic of a given concept; members of a given category may or may not possess all of these features.

Prototype theories: accounts of pattern recognition in which stimuli are recognised by matching to appropriate prototypes (q.v.).

Psychophysics: the study of the relationship between external stimuli and their subjective effects in the form of sensations; a term introduced into psychology by Gustav Fechner.

Rationalisation: as applied to memory, the tendency for story recall to be distorted so as to conform to the cultural conventions and expectations of the rememberer.

Reception paradigm: an experimental procedure in concept learning in which the stimuli presented to the subject are determined by the experimenter; see also Selection paradigm.

Representativeness heuristic: this is a simple strategy used in probability judgements, based on the assumption that representative or typical members of a category are more likely to occur than unrepresentative or atypical ones.

Restricted code: a relatively concrete and descriptive form of language production which can be difficult to understand in the absence of knowledge about the context in which it is used; according to Bernstein, this code is used more by working-class than by middle-class children; see also Elaborated code.

Retrieval: accessing memory traces at the time of a memory test; see also Storage.

Retroactive interference: as applied to memory, the finding that subsequent learning disrupts the memory for previous learning; it is greatest when the stimuli in the two learning tasks are the same but the responses are different; see also Proactive interference.

Retrospective memory: memory of events of the past, in contrast to prospective memory (q.v.).

Rod: receptors mainly in the outer part of the retina of the eye; they are very sensitive to light but do not register colour; see also Cones.

Saccades: rapid movements of the eyes, interspersed with eye fixations.

Schema (plural schemata): large chunks of organised knowledge stored in long-term memory.

Secondary memory: a term introduced by William James to refer to the psychological past or long-term memory.

Selection paradigm: an experimental procedure in concept learning in which the stimuli and their sequencing are determined by the subject; see also Reception paradigm.

Semantic memory: organised knowledge about the world and about language stored in long-term memory; see also Episodic memory.

Semantics: as used by Noam Chomsky, the rules which determine the assignment of meaning to sentences.

Serial processing: processing in which one process is completed before the next process starts; see also Parallel processing.

Signal-detection theory: the view that the absolute threshold (q.v.) and the differential threshold (q.v.) are not fixed at any given value, and that one should distinguish between an individual's sensitivity and his or her cautiousness or response criterion.

Simple cells: cells within the brain which respond maximally to lines having a specific orientation in a specific part of the retina; see also Complex cells and Hypercomplex cells.

Spoonerism: a speech error in which the initial letter or letters of two words are transposed (e.g. "a shoving leopard" instead of "loving shepherd").

Spreading activation theory: the notion that activation of a given concept or word in semantic memory (q.v.) spreads to other concepts, especially those that are closely related in meaning.

Stimulus-driven processing: processing which is determined by an external stimulus rather than by an individual's knowledge and expectations; see also Conceptually driven processing.

Storage: the processes occurring at the time of presentation which lead to information entering long-term memory.

Strategic knowledge: knowledge of the methods which can be used in order to construct an appropriate and coherent writing plan.

Surface structure: a term introduced by Noam Chomsky to refer to the hierarchical division of sentences into their constituent phrases; see also Deep structure.

Syntax: the rules specifying which strings of words are grammatically acceptable within any given language.

Template: miniature copies of previously presented patterns in long-term memory which may be used in pattern recognition.

Three-dimensional model representation: as used by Marr, the end product of visual perception in which the representation is independent of the observer's viewpoint; see also Primal sketch and Two-point-five-dimensional sketch.

Top-down processing: see Conceptually driven processing.

Trace-dependent forgetting: forgetting which occurs because of loss of information from, or decay of, relevant memory traces; see also Cue-dependent forgetting.

Two-point-five-dimensional sketch: as used by Marr, it results from visual perceptual processing, following after the primal sketch (q.v.) and preceding the three-dimensional model representation (q.v.).

Tympanic membrane: the eardrum, from which sound waves travel to the ossicles (q.v.).

Vigilance: an experimental situation in which occasional signals need to be detected in a monotonous and usually long-lasting task.

Vigilance decrement: the finding that performance on vigilance (q.v.) tasks tends to become worse over time.

Working memory: as used by Baddeley and Hitch, a system for active processing and temporary storage of information; it consists of a central executive, an articulatory loop, and a visuo-spatial sketch pad.

Author index

Subject index

magnitude estimation, 17,
177
means-ends analysis, 142,
144, 177
medical information,97-8
memory, 5-7, 9, 67, 127, 138,
150
  absent-mindedness, 60-63
  automatic processing, 56-63,
  174
  forgetting, 89-96
  levels of processing, 77-81
  organisation in, 81-9
  practical applications, 96-100
  short-term/long-term, 68-77
mental imagery, 98-9
mental models, 150-52, 177
mental operators, 139-42, 177
messages (attention), 43-9
method of loci/location, 98
misapplied size-constancy
  theory, 31-2, 177
mnemonic techniques,
  98-100
modules, 6, 7, 177
modus ponens, 145-6, 147-8,
177
modus tollens, 146, 149, 178
morpheme-exchange errors,
121
motion parallax, 30, 178
movement after-effect, 32,
178
multi-store model, 69-70, 71,
77, 78-9, 178

necklace problem, 133-4
negative afterimages, 12, 178
negative transfer effect, 135,
178
neonates (perceptual
  development), 18-19, 21
"noise", 2-3, 16,64
normative decision-making,
159-60

novices, experts &, 137-8

ocular pursuit, 32-3
open-loop mode of control,
  62-3, 178
optic flow patterns, 36, 178
organised perception, 26-35
oscilloscope, 14, 178
ossicles, 15, 178

parallel processing, 4-5, 178
parsing, 112-13
pattern recognition, 33-5, 36
peg systems, 98-9
perception, 11,127
  in infants, 20-24
  theories, 35-9
perceptual cycle, 37-8
perceptual development,
  18-25
perceptual differentiation,
  25, 178
perceptual enrichment
  hypothesis, 25, 178
perceptual organisation,
  26-35
perceptual span, 104-5, 178
permanent memory, 90-92
phonemic restoration effect,
  108-9, 178
phonology, 102, 103, 178
positive transfer effect, 134,
  178
power law of sensory
  intensity, 17
pragmatic reasoning
  schemata, 150, 178
preference task, 20-21
primacy effect, 98
primal sketch, 38, 178
primary memory, 68, 178
proactive interference, 94-6,
  179
probability judgements,
  160-63

problem solving, 131,132-44
problem space, 139-41,179
procedural knowledge, 73-5,
  179
programme assembly
  failures, 62, 63
pronunciation, 106-8
proof-reading, 35
propositions, 117-18
prospective memory, 97, 179
prototype theories, 34,
  155-8, 179
psychophysical functions,
  16-17, 179

rationalisation, 88, 179
reading, 9, 104-8, 111
reasoning, 145-58
recall, 75-6, 81-3, 88, 92-3,
  97-8, 116
reception paradigm, 153, 179
recognition memory, 72-3,
  75-6, 80, 88-9, 92-3, 116,
  157-8
rehearsal process, 69-72,
  78-9, 82-3
reinforcement theory, 102,
  145
representativeness heuristic,
  161-3, 179
repression theory, 93-4
restaurant script, 86-7, 115,
  116
restricted code, 128, 179
retinal image, 22, 23, 28-9,
  30, 31
retrieval, 67, 82-3, 89, 92-3,
  99, 116-17, 179
retroactive interference,
  94-6, 179
retrospective memory, 97,
  179
rhyming recognition test,
  80-81
rods, 12, 13, 179